Managing the Cycle of
Acting-Out Behavior
In the Classroom

Managing the Cycle of
Acting-Out Behavior
In the Classroom

Geoff Colvin

Behavior
Associates
Eugene, Oregon

Cover Design: Christopher Berner, Funk-Levis Associates
Cover Photos: Mark Beardsley and Kylee Colvin
Interior Photos: Mark Beardsley/IRIS Media, Inc. and Kylee Colvin
Interior Design: Bryan Wickman
Editing and Indexing: Tina Wells

ISBN 0-9631777-3-7

Printed in the United States of America.
Published and distributed by:

Behavior
Associates
P.O. Box 5633
Eugene, OR 97405-0633
Tel: (541) 485-6450
Fax: (541) 344-9680

Dedicated to

My wife, Nola
My daughter, Kylee
My exchange daughter from Brazil, Ana

My friend, mentor and inspiration for many years, Zig Engelmann

About the Author

Geoff Colvin, Ph.D., draws on his experience as a teacher, both in special education and in general education, school administrator and research associate at the University of Oregon.

Dr. Colvin is a nationally recognized educational consultant who has assisted personnel in more than 200 school districts and agencies, nationally and internationally, on the subject of managing problem behavior, teaching challenging students and school safety planning. He has authored more than 80 publications including books, book chapters, articles and video programs on teaching and managing students who exhibit the full range of problem behavior. His video program *Defusing Anger and Aggression* received national recognition by winning the 2000 Telly Award and Communicator Award of Distinction.

As an administrator, he directed a juvenile detention school for five years and was the principal for a county–wide school for seriously emotionally disturbed youth for five years. He also served as a supervisor of special programs with Bethel School District, Eugene, Oregon for several years.

Dr. Colvin has a very special skill in being able to translate theory into practice. He is able to present clear explanations and analyses of learning and behavior and at the same time offer concrete examples with hands-on illustrations. His extensive knowledge and experience base, lively speaking style and keen sense of humor have made him a popular speaker at national and international conferences.

Contents

Introduction 1

Section One: A Model 3

    Chapter 1: Analyzing Acting-Out Behavior **4**
    Chapter 2: A Seven-Phase Model for Describing Acting-Out Behavior **12**

Section Two: Strategies 43

    Chapter 3: Proactive Strategies for Maintaining Calm Phase **44**
    Chapter 4: Precorrection Strategies for Triggers Phase **59**
    Chapter 5: Teaching Social Skills for Managing Triggers Phase **72**
    Chapter 6: Calming Strategies for Managing Agitation Phase **86**
    Chapter 7: Defusing Strategies for Managing Acceleration Phase **98**
    Chapter 8: Safe Management Strategies for Peak Phase **114**
    Chapter 9: Reintegration Strategies for De-escalation Phase **125**
    Chapter 10: Resumption Strategies for Recovery Phase **134**

Section Three: Conclusion 143

    Chapter 11: Summary and Case Study **144**

Appendices 149

    Appendix A–O, Reproducible Checklists, Plans and Forms

References 165

Author Index 171

Subject Index 173

Credits 179

INTRODUCTION

Acting-out behavior manifests itself in many different ways in classroom settings such as running away, physical aggression, verbal abuse, serious confrontations and threats, sexual acting-out, criminal behavior such as vandalism, defiance and non-compliance, tantrums and many different forms of anger. While these behaviors may differ in their form, settings and outcomes, there are several common factors. For example, some students may be angry towards their parents or particular teachers and skip school, vandalize shops in the neighborhood or become hostile towards their teachers and get suspended from school. Clearly, each of these behaviors is different, but they are all motivated by anger towards their parents or teachers. Other students may become depressed, lose their confidence and become sexually active, stop eating or give up on their schoolwork. Again the responses are very different yet each student is attempting to deal with depression, albeit in ways that are essentially self-destructive and very counterproductive.

In this book acting-out behavior will be used along with other descriptors for students displaying serious problem behavior, especially explosive and escalating behavior. Other descriptors for these students include antisocial, behavior disordered and troubled students.

The book is divided into three sections. The purpose of the first section is to describe the development and detail of a conceptual model for acting-out behavior. An analysis of an acting-out behavioral cycle is presented followed by a description of a model comprised of seven clearly defined phases. Common behavioral features are delineated for each phase in the model which allows staff to develop a specific behavior profile for a student with acting-out behavior problems. Once this profile, or assessment, has been made staff is in a strong position to develop a comprehensive behavior plan to interrupt the cycle of acting-out behavior and to establish appropriate behavior.

The second section, which constitutes the bulk of the book, is devoted to an explanation and description of many strategies for managing each of the seven phases in the acting-out cycle. The strategies selected are taken from research and best practice procedures reported in the literature and practiced in the field. Since each phase represents a link in the behavioral chain, staff's effective management of the behaviors in the early phases of the behavior chain may preempt the later phases where the more serious behaviors occur. Emphasis is placed on teaching and prevention techniques in the early phases. In the latter phases, the approach is to stress safety, crisis management, re-entry and follow-up procedures.

In the third and final section, the procedures for managing the cycle of acting-out behavior are summarized followed by a case study. The case study is presented to illustrate the assessment features paired with strategies for each phase in the acting-out cycle.

The reader is referred to an Appendix section at the back of the book. This section contains all of the forms presented throughout the book. These forms may be reproduced or adapted for personal use in the classroom.

Section One—

A Model

General education teachers have to deal with ever increasing numbers of students who are difficult to manage and teach. In addition, teachers are discovering that the management practices that have worked so well over the years with typical students do not seem to be very effective with these more difficult students. In fact, teachers often report that such practices often make the situation worse, especially with students who exhibit acting-out or explosive forms of behavior. The teacher, for example, asks a student to pick up some paper that was thrown on the floor. The student responds with some bad language. Now the teacher has to deal with the bad language, in addition to the issue of the paper thrown on the floor.

Sometimes a teacher's strategy may be effective in calming down a student, but, in the process, may inadvertently reinforce the problem behavior. Consequently, the next time students encounter a similar situation, they will be more likely to exhibit the initial problem behavior so as to receive the attention and responses from the teacher.

The purpose of Section One is to provide understanding of the nature of acting-out behavior. With more careful and detailed analysis of this behavior, there is more chance of using strategies that may be effective in changing the behavior and less chance of using strategies that may escalate the situation. In Chapter 1, an analysis of acting-out behavior is provided followed by Chapter 2 in which a specific seven-phase model is described.

Chapter 1

Analyzing Acting-Out Behavior

In order to understand the acting-out behavior cycle, it is helpful to closely examine a specific, typical example. An example will be presented followed by an in-depth review of the major factors that were significant in this acting-out episode. These factors become the cornerstone for the seven-phase model presented in the next chapter and the basis for many of the strategies described in Section Two. Topics to be addressed include: *(a)* Example of acting-out behavior; *(b)* Prerequisite academic skills; *(c)* Signs of agitation; *(d)* Presence of an escalating behavior chain; and *(e)* Presence of successive interactions.

Example of Acting-Out Behavior Cycle

In the following example, a student in a typical classroom exhibits a range of behaviors in an acting-out cycle. The setting and interactions between the teacher and student are described in Box 1.1.

Box 1.1: Example of the Cycle of Acting-Out Behavior

During independent work in math, students are expected to complete problems that were assigned in the previous class. One student, Michael, is sitting slouched in his seat, feet stretched out, arms folded, head down, staring down at the floor, and looking very serious. The successive interactions are presented along with a brief description of the teacher and student's behavior.

Teacher	Michael
"Michael, it is time to get started with your math." *In a pleasant manner*	"What math?" *In a somewhat surly manner*
"The math you didn't finish this morning." *Somewhat matter-of-fact manner*	"I did finish it!" *Gruffly*

Box 1.1 Continued

"Well, let me see your work, please." *Pleasantly*

"Good, you have done four problems but you need to do ten." *In matter-of-fact manner*

"I announced that at the beginning of class yesterday." *Firmly*

"Michael, look at the board. See under assignment, one through ten." *Quite firmly*

"Look Michael. This has gone far enough. You need to finish the rest of your assignment. So please get on with it." *Very firmly*

"OK. Here is your choice. Do the math now or you will have to do it during the break." *Clearly and resolutely*

"That's verbal abuse. I will now do an office referral." *Somewhat agitated*

"All right. It's to the Office." *Nudges student on the elbow.*

Teacher follows emergency procedures and calls for help resulting in student being escorted to the Office.

Michael leans back. *Reluctantly*

"When did we have to do ten?" *In belligerent tone*

"I don't remember that!" *Belligerently*

"Well that's the first time I've seen it." *Very firmly*

"No way. I'm not doing any more!" *Loudly and resolutely*

"F… you." *Offensively and insolently*

Stands up and throws book across the room. *Very agitated*

Swings arm in direction of teacher and makes solid contact with teacher's arm.

Source: Walker, Colvin, & Ramsey, *1995.*

Emergency procedures in most schools typically require the teacher to submit an incident report as part of the follow-up procedures. In this case the teacher's report is presented in Box 1.2.

> **Box 1.2: Incident Report**
>
> The class was finishing a Math assignment and Michael was just sitting there doing nothing. I approached him to see if he needed help. He was very uncooperative and began to argue. He was quite surly. He had made a start and I directed him to continue his work and finish the assignment. He refused to work, saying he is not going to do any more. I followed my usual procedure of giving him a choice of working now or doing it during the break. He cussed me out saying, "F… you." I started to fill out an office referral and he stood up and threw his book against the wall, showing a lot of anger. I was worried about the safety of other students and proceeded to direct him to the office. At this point, he swung his arm very hard and hit me causing considerable pain. I sent for help immediately.

Initially, the person following through on this incident, usually an administrator, would focus on one aspect of this report, specifically, the issue of the student hitting the teacher. While there were several behaviors of concern exhibited by Michael such as non-compliance, disrespect and verbal abuse, hitting the teacher was much more serious. The administrator may need to call the police, suspend the student, or call for a parent conference depending on the degree of the incident, or the harmful effects of the student's hitting behavior. The usual sequence following such an incident as hitting the teacher is to:

1. Isolate the student

2. Allow time for the student to calm down

3. Interview the student

4. Deliver a consequence such as suspension or detention and a parent conference

5. Specify a re-entry plan that might involve a student-teacher meeting, follow-up by the student requiring an apology, and statement of commitment to avoid any further incidents of hitting staff or others

6. Resume the regular schedule

These actions taken by the administrator may effectively prevent future occurrences of hitting by the student. However, the other behaviors leading up to the hitting are not addressed. Consequently, Michael may, more than likely, exhibit these behaviors in the near future. We have an example of a *behavior chain* here and the only behavior addressed is the one at the end of the chain, specifically, hitting the teacher. The behaviors early in the chain are not addressed, making it likely that there will be further occurrences of these behaviors. In other words a situation may arise again with Michael wherein he engages in all of the behaviors in this chain and stops short of hitting the teacher. Granted the teacher does not want to be hit, but neither does the teacher want to be faced with all of these other inappropriate behaviors.

Thus, we are faced with a critical question, "What needs to be done to prevent this *whole scene* from happening again?" In effect, "How can we interrupt this behavior chain or prevent it from ever getting started? There are four essential components that need to be understood and addressed if we are to be successful in managing this behavior chain effectively:

1. Prerequisite academic skills
2. Signs of agitation
3. Presence of an escalating behavior chain
4. Presence of successive interactions

Prerequisite Academic Skills

There are many reasons why a student may struggle to begin work, refuse to work, or begin work and then stop. It could be that the student cannot understand the assignment, or lacks the skills to complete the work, or already has complete mastery of the subject and is now bored with it. Perhaps the student is having a bad day and is distracted by some serious problems. Maybe the student is feeling unwell or possibly angry with the teacher for some other reason and is just not going to cooperate this day. Usually a teacher does not have time, in the context of teaching a whole class of students, to carefully and systematically investigate why it is that the student is not on task. However, the safest and perhaps most efficient way of getting started in this investigation is to ensure that the student understands the work and has the necessary skills to get started, stay on task, and complete the assignment. Consequently, the teacher would initially focus on the *prerequisite academic skills* for completing the assignment. If the teacher addresses other variables that may cause disturbance, the student will still not be able to complete the task if the necessary academic skills are not present. However, once the issue of academic competence for the assignment has been addressed, the teacher is then in a stronger position to examine other variables that may be contributing to the student's unrest. Several strategies designed to address academic skills and to increase on-task behavior are presented in Chapter 3.

Signs of Agitation

The body language presented by Michael, even before the teacher approached him, showed every sign that he was on edge. The slouched position, feet outstretched, arms folded, head down staring at the floor and basically motionless were all indicators that he was quite upset over something and that it would only be a matter of time before he would escalate. In addition, his very first response to the teacher's request for him to resume his assignment was, "What math?" spoken in a surly manner. This response also indicated that he was having problems. However, the teacher basically stayed with the issue of getting on with his work and Michael's agitated state was not addressed. What might have been the outcome had the teacher addressed his agitation with a comment like, "Are you doing OK?" or "Do you need some time?" In these cases, there could have been a very good chance that Michael may have felt supported and calmed down to some extent. In this way, the escalated sequence could have been prevented and the student may have settled down to focus on his work.

Agitation is a critical variable in the cycle of acting-out behavior and detailed information for identifying the signs of agitation will be presented later in Chapter 2. Several strategies will be described for reducing agitation in Chapter 6.

Presence of an Escalating Behavior Chain

Once the teacher approached Michael and prompted him to begin his assignment, Michael responded with a question ("What math?"). The teacher answered the question, which set the stage for Michael to challenge the teacher and ask more questions. We see this pattern of questioning and arguing continue until the teacher gives an explicit direction to start work. Michael then refuses, displaying non-compliant and defiant behavior, ("No way, I'm not doing any more!"). The teacher presents Michael with a choice of working now or on his own time, to which Michael responds with verbal abuse. Shortly after, Michael stands up, throws a book, and ultimately hits the teacher. This whole process can be described as an escalating *behavior chain,* see Figure 1.1, where each ensuing behavior is more serious than the one preceding it leading to the last one, the most serious of all where Michael hits the teacher.

A critical question becomes, "What if Michael's questioning and arguing behavior were terminated early through different management strategies?" The most likely outcome would be that there would be nothing to set the stage for the next behavior, non-compliance. Similarly, if non-compliance were not present there would be nothing to set the stage for teacher verbal abuse and finally assault. In other words, if this chain were interrupted at an early stage, there would be nothing to prompt the more serious forms of behavior occurring at the end of the chain. In effect, the teacher assault and preceding serious behaviors would have been prevented.

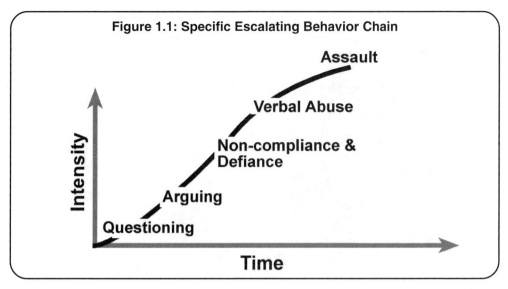

Figure 1.1: Specific Escalating Behavior Chain

There is a very simple assumption regarding behavior chains and that is each behavior needs to be prompted by a preceding behavior. If the preceding behavior is not present, or interrupted, then the next behavior will not occur.

The successive stages in an escalating behavior chain in relation to a conceptual model are described below and in Chapter 2. In Chapters 4 and 5, specific strategies will be presented for intervening early in the chain and defusing the situation.

Presence of Successive Interactions

It is very clear that in the current example Michael was engaged in an escalating behavior chain. Moreover, when we review the office report, Michael did indeed exhibit very serious behavior that warranted immediate action by school authorities. However, the specific dynamics of the teacher's behavior are only implied. In fact, at first glance the teacher's responses to Michael's on-going behavior problems seemed quite reasonable and representative of what most teachers would do in this situation, specifically:

1. Prompting an off-task student to begin work
2. Presenting a clear direction to break up the on-going arguing and questioning
3. Providing a choice in the face of non-compliance
4. Writing an office referral for verbal abuse
5. Trying to have a student leave the room when the situation looked very serious

Successive interactions between teacher and student.

However, in the situation we are really looking at a series of interactions involving both teacher and student behavior. For each student behavior, there is a corresponding or reciprocal teacher behavior. In other words, each successive student behavior is preceded by a specific teacher behavior. Or, it could be argued, that each teacher behavior is preceded by a specific student behavior. In this sense, we may conclude that the teacher behavior may have set the stage for the next student behavior and that the student behavior set the stage for the next teacher behavior. These successive interactions can be described as a series of, "My turn-your turn" events. For example, Michael is off task (Michael's turn) and the teacher prompts him to start work (Teacher's turn). Michael questions and argues (Michael's turn) and the teacher gives an explicit direction to start work (Teacher's turn). Michael refuses to start work (Michael's turn) and the teacher gives him a choice between doing the work now or doing it at recess (Teacher's turn) and this pattern continues leading to Michael hitting the teacher.

Now a critical question arises with this example, "What if the teacher did not take a turn?" Theoretically there would be nothing to set the stage for Michael's next behavior. By not responding, the teacher may effectively terminate Michael's behavior. The chain would be broken or interrupted. A crucial component for managing this kind of problem behavior is to fully recognize the role of successive interactions in escalating behavior patterns, especially the role of teacher behavior. Essentially the teacher behavior determines the kind of behavior exhibited by the student. If the teacher behavior displays escalation, then the student behavior will surely escalate.

Geoff Colvin

Some teacher behaviors will escalate student behavior; other teacher behaviors may defuse the situation. In Chapters 4 and 5, an array of teacher responses will be described that are designed to defuse the situation avoiding escalating student behavior.

Summary

An example of serious acting-out behavior was described in detail. It was evident as the episode unfolded that a number of factors came into play. The incident involved an escalation of behavior in which the level of intensity of the student's behavior increased from resistant behavior to serious unsafe behavior. These increases in behavior can be described in terms of an escalating chain of behavior with observable, discrete stages. This concept is developed more fully in Chapter 2 where a seven-phase model for describing the cycle of acting-out behavior is presented.

Several factors were identified as key events or circumstances that may have significantly contributed to escalating the student's behavior. The important implication is that if these factors were addressed in a systematic manner, the escalating chain of behavior involving Michael and his teacher may have been avoided or prevented. Details for each of these strategies will be described more fully in Section Two, Chapters 3 through 8.

Chapter 2

A Seven-Phase Model for Describing Acting-Out Behavior

The escalated behavior pattern for the teacher-student interaction in the previous example, and the de-escalated pattern can be described in seven phases (Colvin, 1992; Kauffman, Mostert, Trent, & Hallahan, 1998; Sprague & Golly, 2004). The specific phases that describe the successive student behaviors in the cycle are depicted in Figure 2.1. Note that the graph rises as the interaction escalates and falls away as the student behavior de-escalates. The escalating behaviors are depicted in phases one through five, followed by the de-escalating behaviors in phases six and seven. In general, this conceptual model represents the interdependent behavioral dynamics of the student behavior during an escalating and de-escalating interaction.

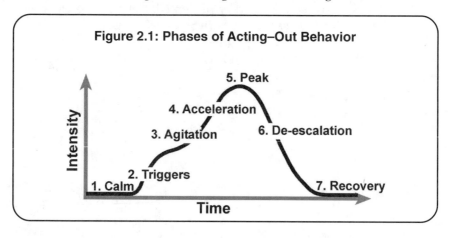

Figure 2.1: Phases of Acting–Out Behavior

Teachers, on-line staff, parents and peers are often unwittingly trapped in escalating interactions with antisocial students that prove to be very disruptive, damaging to relationships, and in some cases, extremely dangerous. Antisocial students carry high levels of *agitation* due to the many and varied stresses they are under which are often exacerbated by the neglect and abuse from settings outside of school (Patterson, 1988; Patterson, Reid, & Dishion, 1992; Walker, Colvin, & Ramsey, 1995; Walker, Stieber, Ramsey, O'Neill, & Eisert, 1994). This agitation serves as a fuel that drives a coercive behavioral process that is often triggered by seemingly innocuous events such as asking questions, making requests, giving directions and, especially, delivering consequences for inappropriate behavior. Once triggered, subsequent explosive behavior is difficult to curtail and can lead to serious behavior.

Figure 2.1 illustrates the escalation and de-escalation processes involved in this highly coercive process. Understanding this phenomenon is essential to managing the intense behavioral challenges presented by these students with serious problem behavior.

The specific content has been derived from the author's experience from observing and working with numerous antisocial students over the past twenty-five years and from reviewing research literature and published best practice procedures. Typical behavioral characteristics are presented that are associated with student responses to each of the seven phases identified in this acting-out cycle. In many cases, these cycles involve an escalated interaction between the teacher and student that is intense, explosive, and often unsafe. Moreover these students may engage in these seven phases during an episode and subsequently exhibit relatively normal behavior for a few days or even a few weeks. However, depending on the presence of the triggers, the problem behavioral pattern may resurface. It is for this reason that the pattern is called an acting-out *cycle.*

Each cycle can be described in terms of seven phases:

1. Calm
2. Triggers
3. Agitation
4. Acceleration
5. Peak
6. De-escalation
7. Recovery

A detailed description now follows for the behavioral characteristics of each of the seven phases; a summary behavioral description of each phase; an illustration for each phase; and a summary check-list for the acting-out behavior cycle.

PHASE ONE—CALM

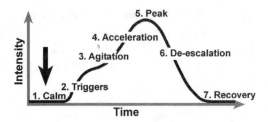

Angry and aggressive students are relatively calm in the initial phase of the acting-out behavior cycle. To all outward appearances, their behavior is appropriate, generally cooperative, and responsive to the teacher's directions and expectations.

Teachers often report that the student was having a good day (at least the level of behavior was such that instruction could take place and the student was learning or engaged in the classroom activities). It is quite common, at a staff meeting called for one of these students, for a teacher to report that, "Most of the time, 'Student's name' is a delight to have in the classroom but at other times he is a totally different person." These students are able to function appropriately with other students in regard to sharing, working together and getting along in general. They are able to respond appropriately to praise and show interest and satisfaction in getting their work done and achieving their goals. Essentially, the students behave and respond in the manner of other students exhibiting the behavioral expectations of the classroom. Keep in mind, though, that these students may never be "role models" for behavior compared to other students. However, on many occasions they can engage appropriately in classroom activities for extended periods of time and participate, to an adequate degree, in the normal events of the classroom.

Phase One:
Relatively calm.

Photo by: Kylee Colvin

Geoff Colvin

Example of Student Behavior during Calm Phase. An illustration of a student's behavior for Phase One, *Calm*, is presented in Box 2.1.

Box 2.1: Illustration of Student Behavior in Phase One—*Calm*

Robert entered the classroom chatting to another student and went to his desk and sat down. Some of the other students started to get their materials out and Robert watched one of these students somewhat closely. He then opened his own desk-top and began to pull out some books and materials. Most of the students began to do the math puzzle that was on the overhead projector. Robert sat there and was looking around. The teacher noticed he hadn't commenced work and said, "Robert let's get started on the math puzzle please." Robert muttered OK and began to work on the puzzle. He then stopped and looked at what the student next to him was doing. The student told him that you just have to join the lines and it will tell you the answer. So Robert began to join the lines. The class was expected to turn in the puzzle to the teacher and then begin some quiet reading until everyone was finished. Robert eventually finished and the teacher thanked him for getting the work done. Robert smiled. He went to another student and the teacher reminded him to go to his desk and begin some quiet reading. Robert said nothing but went to his desk and opened a book. At that moment the teacher said, "OK everyone, I want you to put your reading book away now and watch here please." Robert, along with the class put his reading book away and looked at his teacher.

In this scenario, it was clear that Robert was not fully engaged with the class activity in that he needed help to start the puzzle, was slow to finish and, at one point, needed a reminder from the teacher to sit down and begin reading. However, his behavior was sufficiently acceptable for him to be maintained in the classroom and would be regarded as someone who needs structure and assistance on a regular basis.

Characteristics of Students in the Calm Phase

During this phase the students are able to exhibit, in varying degrees, the essential behaviors to succeed in class. These behaviors include: *(a)* Maintaining on-task behavior; *(b)* Following rules and expectations; *(c)* Responding to praise; *(d)* Initiating appropriate behavior; and *(e)* Responding to goals and success.

Summary of Phase One—Calm

Overall behavior is cooperative and acceptable.

Phase Two—Triggers

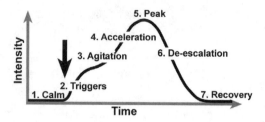

Triggers are defined as those events that set off the cycle of acting-out behavior. The student may be engaged appropriately in the first phase, *calm*, and a trigger comes into play that sets the stage for acting-out behavior. For example, the student needs help with a problem and another student says, "Gees dummy. Can't you do that!" The student then becomes very agitated and moves towards the one who made the offensive remark. Other names for triggers include:

- Setting events
- Aversive stimuli
- Antecedents
- Past history
- Negative circumstances

The triggers serve to increase the agitation level of the student, giving rise to the beginning of an acting-out cycle. In general there are two types of triggers operating in this phase: *(a)* School-based; and *(b)* Nonschool-based.

School-Based Triggers

Conflicts. The sources of student conflicts occurring at school fall into two broad categories: *(a)* Denial of something the student wants or needs; and *(b)* Something negative is inflicted on the student. In the first place, students who exhibit serious acting-out behavior typically do not have good communication skills. Consequently, when they need something, their limited verbal skills often do not allow them to communicate what they need appropriately, if at all. For example, they might yell out in class that they need a pencil, which is an unacceptable response for the teacher. If students perceive their needs as being denied, they often react in an angry manner and may receive negative consequences for their inappropriate behavior. Consequently, the initial need is not met and the student ends up in trouble for reacting in an inappropriate manner which is highly likely to set the stage for further escalation.

In the second case these students, who are easily triggered, are often provoked by a perception that something negative is inflicted upon them.

Student conflict in hallway.

Source: IRIS Media, Inc.

For example, another student may bump into them, refuse to give them something, not allow them to join in a game, or call them names, even in a joking manner. These students then react inappropriately to the perceived negative events and may receive consequences for their reaction. Students with acting-out behavior can readily become frustrated under such conditions as they perceive the situation as not being their fault to begin with and yet they are the ones receiving the penalties. The situation is further exacerbated if the other students are seen as receiving no consequences for their role in the problem. In effect these students see the situation as unfair which may cause further reactions leading to serious escalation.

Student triggers at recess.

Source: IRIS Media, Inc.

Changes in Routine. These students with acting-out behavior often react negatively to sudden changes in routines, especially if the activity is something that has fully engaged them or something they haven't quite finished. Transitions from one setting to another or from one activity to another are difficult for these students. Other adaptations, such as a change in schedule or adjustments made to rules, can upset these students, even when the changes are clearly recognizable. Similarly, acting-out students typically have trouble adapting to substitute teachers. In general, these students have trouble adjusting to changes and may respond with inappropriate reactions leading to escalation.

Peer Provocations. Unfortunately, other students sometimes see these easily triggered students as *fair game.* Consequently, these peers can very predictably cause their readily triggered peers to escalate and get into trouble through provocations, such as name calling, teasing, interfering with their activities or belongings, or making fun of them in the presence of other peers. Under these conditions the students with acting-out behavior may react and the situation will more than likely escalate to serious behavior.

Pressure. School can be viewed as a very high-demand situation in which students are expected to comply with a wide variety of directions and complete a number of often complex tasks during the course of a school day. Students are expected to manage their time well, function independently in a number of situations and often to manage multiple tasks at the same time. In many cases, the students with serious problem behavior do not have the skills necessary to meet these expectations, consequently they feel they are under constant pressure. The seemingly ordinary demands of a school day can set the stage for panic, depression, anxiety and other emotional responses resulting in poor decisions and leading to additional problems.

Ineffective Problem Solving. Acting-out students generally have limited strategies for identifying sources of problems, generating adaptive options, evaluating them, negotiating with others, and implementing plans accordingly. These students often apply one ineffective strategy repeatedly or resort to angry reactive behavior. They have not learned how to solve problems systematically and essentially they need formal and systematic teaching in these areas.

Facing Errors during Instruction. In many cases, these students will stop working after they make errors and will avoid new learning rather than make more mistakes. Their self-confidence is very fragile because of overall lack of success in schoolwork. Consequently, when they face new or challenging work, or make errors, the situation can escalate to serious acting-out behavior or lead to avoidance of the work.

Facing Correction Procedures. Easily triggered students often have problems in accepting assistance after errors have been made or with being required to do the task over again. Teacher corrections and debriefings (standard procedures for the teaching and learning process) may actually prompt substantial increases in their agitation levels. Moreover, it becomes very difficult for the teacher to engage these students in new learning (an essential goal of instruction and academic achievement) because of the problems the students have in dealing with errors and corrections.

Nonschool-Based Triggers

High Needs Homes. Students who have behavior disorders often come from homes where many critical needs are not met. At an early age they may experience poverty, which can lead to serious neglect issues regarding adequate shelter, food, support and nurturing. The parents through unemployment, forced transience and poverty are not in a position to provide a stable and nurturing home environment that is necessary for healthy personal, social and emotional growth in their children. The intent here is not to criticize parents, rather to point out that the overwhelming stresses that many parents face on a daily basis can pose serious limitations to meet their needs and their capacity to raise healthy and adjusted children.

Some parents, sadly, are guilty of child abuse which directly contributes to acting-out behavior. Abused children are obvious candidates for antisocial behaviors.

Health Problems. Unfortunately, in our society, there are many parents who do not have health insurance or may have very limited insurance coupled with low income. This means that an appointment with a doctor could use up several days' income. On-going medical treatment for their children is almost out of the question. Over-the-counter remedies may also be too costly. These parents may find a way to manage the more serious sicknesses of their children through various assistance programs or family support, but often cannot address the common or chronic illnesses such as viruses, infections, headaches, cramping, hay fever and asthma. Consequently, these children may come to school sick because their parents cannot afford the necessary treatment nor be able to stay home with them. There is no question that student behaviors are different when the students are healthy compared to when they are sick.

Nutrition Needs. One of the most serious outcomes for families afflicted with poverty is that the children (and adults for that matter) do not have regular, well-balanced meals and are often hungry. School supported lunch and breakfast programs help address this problem. However, the children do not have access to these meals on weekends and school holidays. Deficits in nutrition not only impact on health and general well-being, but may also seriously and adversely affect student behavior.

Inadequate Sleep. Sleeping patterns of many students are often irregular and inadequate. Environmental factors that may contribute to sleeping problems for students include excitement before sleep, going to bed too late from watching TV or engaging in other activities, excessive noise in the household or neighborhood, and crowded conditions and conflicts that arise regularly. In addition there are physical or medical issues that may keep a child awake including the side-effects of medication, chronic illnesses such as headaches or stomach upsets, anxiety, and active minds. Children need adequate rest to function appropriately in school and inadequate sleep makes it very difficult for children to behave appropriately and to participate effectively during instruction and other school activities.

Dual Diagnoses. In some cases children are given dual diagnoses and the respective treatments may interact negatively with each other. For example, a student may receive the dual diagnosis of attention deficit disorder and oppositional disorder. The typical treatment is prescribed medication. In many cases there are side-effects to the medication that may cause agitation or discomfort to the student giving rise to problem behavior. Moreover, the prescriptions are often *experimental* in that the levels of dosage or the kind of medication prescribed is based on the child's response to the medication. During this period of on-going adjustments of the medication, the student may exhibit problem behavior.

Substance Abuse. Students who use drugs and alcohol often exhibit serious and unpredictable acting-out behavior at school. Similarly, if they have been deprived of the controlled substances, for whatever reason, problem behavior will arise because of the effects of withdrawal. Moreover, a growing population of children are born to substance-addicted mothers, causing alarming effects on these children in physical and social-emotional areas. The problems of agitation and other related disorders presented by these children make them extremely challenging to teach and manage in school.

Gangs and Deviant Peer Groups. Membership in gangs and deviant peer groups sets the stage for serious problems at school, especially with school authority and peer relationships. Membership is also associated with criminal behavior and inattendance at school. The safety of the school community becomes a salient issue with membership in these deviant groups.

Compound Triggers

While the triggers have been presented in two groups, school-based and nonschool-based, some students with serious problem behavior experience these triggers in both settings. This means that the triggers may not be a single event, such as teasing at school. Rather, several triggers may be operative, arising from both school and outside of school. In these situations, the triggers need to be seen as a series of events having a cumulative effect, which may account for the explosiveness of the behaviors in some cases.

Example of Phase Two Triggers. An illustration of the *Triggers* experienced by a student is presented in Box 2.2.

Box 2.2: Illustration of Phase Two—*Triggers*

Mary-Jo did not have a good night at home. She had a big argument with her older sister over whose turn it was to clean up the kitchen. Her sister made her clean up the kitchen when their mom was not home, and when their mom got home her sister claimed to have cleaned up the kitchen. The two girls began yelling at each other so loudly that their mom sent them both to their rooms. Mary-Jo was extremely upset as she thought her sister was lying and now she is in trouble and has to sit in her room all night. She was so mad this time that she couldn't get to sleep till quite late, and when morning came around she was very tired and upset and didn't want to go to school. Her mom told her she was not sick and must go to school. While Mary-Jo was waiting in line at her classroom door, another girl pushed in ahead of her. Mary-Jo said quite loudly that she was there first and the other girl said she was not, just as loudly. At that moment the teacher opened the door and heard the yelling. The teacher told both girls that yelling is not OK and directed each of them to go to the end of the line. Mary-Jo and the girl started pushing each other to avoid being last in line. The girl called Mary-Jo a name. Mary-Jo became very angry and pushed the girl hard enough to knock her down. The teacher saw the girl get pushed over and sent Mary-Jo to the Office for hitting.

Trigger Phase: Student corrected in presence of peers.

Source: IRIS Media, Inc.

In this example the student experiences triggers at home and at school. At home she is wronged by her sister and yet they both get into trouble with her mom. Similarly at school, she feels a victim as a student cut in line resulting in both of them being sent to the end of the line. Moreover, the girl calls Mary-Jo a name, making her mad enough to retaliate by pushing, resulting in her being sent to the office.

None of the triggers are effectively resolved for the student so that each successive trigger from home to school builds more and more anxiety or frustration for the student. Ultimately, the student explodes and hits another student.

> **Summary of Phase Two—Triggers**
> Overall behavior involves a series of unresolved problems.

Phase Three—Agitation

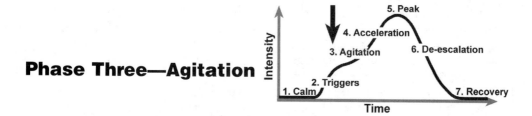

Once the Phase Two triggers begin to take effect, the student moves from the Calm phase to Phase Three, Agitation. Agitation is a general behavioral term, or response class, that includes emotional dispositions such as being angry, upset, depressed, on-edge, withdrawn, worried, disturbed, frustrated and anxious. Students often display high levels of agitation as a function of their inability to control or manage the triggers identified in Phase Two.

The Agitation phase can last for a considerable amount of time, depending on the events that take place or on which stimuli are present. Teachers may describe these students as "being on edge" and that it does not take much to tip them over the edge. The graph in Figure 2.1 flattens out to illustrate the potential of a longer duration in this phase. In general, agitation can be manifested in one of two ways: (a) Responses indicating *increases* in behavior; or, (b) Responses indicating *decreases* in behavior. It is very important to note that the behaviors exhibited in this phase represent *changes* from the behaviors in the previous phase, Calm. If the student exhibits these behaviors habitually, then we are looking at a very different problem, such as hyperactivity or severe depression or psychotic conditions.

Geoff Colvin

Increases in Behavior

Darting Eyes. Students look here and look there with a certain level of intensity but with little focus or purpose to their eye movements. Their eyes appear to fully engage and then they shift to somewhere else.

Busy Hands. Students often display a noticeable increase in hand movements, such as pencil tapping, drumming fingers, rubbing their thighs, opening and closing books, and tugging at their clothes. The behaviors resemble those of a student with hyperactivity except that the student does not exhibit these behaviors during the Calm phase. This behavior is very prevalent among students with severe disabilities especially in the area of language and communication.

Moving In and Out of Groups. These students will want to join a group and when they do, they want to join another group or do something else. They act as if they do not know what they want or that nothing seems to engage their attention for very long.

Off-Task and On-Task Cycle. Similarly, they will start a task or activity and then stop, and then start up again. There appears to be little, if any, fixed or sustained attention to academic tasks or classroom activities. They appear to be pre-occupied.

Decreases in Behavior

Staring into Space. Students appear to be daydreaming and staring into space. They seem to be looking at something with a certain amount of concentration but their minds are somewhere else. They may also appear to be "deaf" in that things are said to them but they do not give any indication that they have heard anything.

Veiled Eyes. The students will avoid eye contact by looking away or looking down. Similarly, they will pull their hat down over their eyes or pull up the lapels of their jacket and sink their head as low into the jacket as they can.

Nonconversational Language. Student responses are such that it is difficult to build a conversation. For example, the teacher may greet the student and say, "Hi Tony, how was your weekend?" He responds quite tersely, "Fine." The teacher then says, "What did you do?" Tony answers while looking away, "Nothing." Essentially the student is communicating that he does not wish to chat.

In some cases the student's delivery is very subdued and difficult to hear. Again the student is communicating that he or she is not wanting to engage in conversation.

Contained Hands. By contrast to the other group where busy hands were a signal of agitation, this group may hide their hands by sitting on them, folding their arms or putting their hands behind their back. Essentially, these students contain their hands as a strategy for disengaging from present academic tasks or classroom activities.

Withdrawal from Groups. The students show a tendency to withdraw from the group, shut down, engage in independent activities or move to isolated areas. There is the clear communication, "Leave me alone."

Example of Phase Three, Agitation. An illustration of Phase Three, *Agitation*, is presented in Box 2.3.

Box 2.3: Illustration of Phase Three—*Agitation*

Sarah came into class with a very serious look on her face. She brushed past some students who greeted her but she kept walking to her desk. The teacher said good morning to her and she mumbled something that could not be heard. She then sat down with her feet stretched out on the floor, sank down into her desk and stared at the floor. The teacher asked the class to take out their homework. The class began to open their bags and pull out their books while Sarah continued to sit there looking at the floor. The teacher noticed Sarah had not responded and approached her saying, "Sarah, it's time to get out your homework please." At this point, Sarah gave a slight start and said, "What was that?" The teacher said quietly, "Homework." Sarah said, "Oh" and began to look through her backpack. The teacher moved looking somewhat puzzled because it took three tries to get Sarah to pull out her homework.

Agitation Phase: Student reacting to correction.

Photo by: Kylee Colvin

Geoff Colvin

In this example, Sarah is showing several signs that she is agitated by her body language, failure to respond to the other students, seeking to isolate herself at her desk, and her failure to attend to the teacher's first two directions to get out her homework. It is clear she has something on her mind and with some students it may not take much to escalate their behavior when they are displaying this level of agitation.

> **Summary of Phase Three—Agitation**
> Overall behavior is unfocused and distracted.

Phase Four—Acceleration

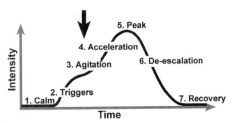

At first glance of the *Acceleration* Phase, Figure 2.1, there is little difference between this phase and the previous phase, agitation. However, there is a marked difference between the two phases in terms of the focus of the student behavior and outcomes of these behaviors. The previous phase characterizes students who are unfocused and the behavior is nondirected. The student is basically saying, "Leave me alone." However, in this phase, acceleration, student behavior becomes quite focused and directed (usually towards staff). In this phase the student is saying, "I want to engage you." In other words, the students exhibit *engaging* behavior that is highly likely to obtain a response from another person, typically the teacher. Following are a number of behaviors students exhibit that have this feature of engaging some other person.

Questioning and Arguing. Students set themselves up to need help or ask questions and then proceed to argue about the responses or details of the task given to them. Generally, the student is not seeking assistance or essential information but rather setting the stage for confrontation with the teacher.

Noncompliance and Defiance. Here the students refuse to cooperate, usually in response to teacher directions, demands or classroom rules and expectations. For example, the teacher may direct the class to clear their desks and get ready for math. For example, Jamal just sits there without clearing his desk. The teacher reminds him to clear his desk and he mutters, "I'm not doing math." The stage is now set for confrontation or further negative interactions. Other common noncooperative or challenging student responses include, "No way," "Make me," "That's not fair," and "You can't make me do nothing." Nonverbal responses are also used, such as staring at the teacher, turning aside, walking away, putting head down, closing eyes or covering ears.

Off-Task Behavior. Teachers have a general expectation that students should be on task or engaged in academic tasks and classroom activities. Thus, when students are not on task teachers usually address the situation by providing a reminder, checking their work, or offering assistance. Once the teacher approaches, however, the student will engage in more avoidance behavior or other inappropriate behavior to further engage the teacher.

Two students off task.

Source: IRIS Media, Inc.

Provocation of Others. Students sometimes exhibit behaviors that irritate others and cause them to react strongly. These behaviors are likened to "pressing buttons." The student knows in advance what will cause the other person (staff, students or family) to react. Once the reaction occurs, especially if it is a strong one, the stage is set for further negative interactions. Examples of provocative behavior include name calling, teasing, put-downs, insults, racial slurs, harassment and interfering with other people's property or activities.

Compliance with Accompanying Inappropriate Behavior. This behavioral event, which is a form of limit testing, has two components: (*a*) Students actually complete the task or follow the direction; and also (*b*) Exhibit additional social behavior that is unacceptable. For example, Ginger may be asked to sit down which she does, (compliance), but at the same time bangs her book on the desk (additional unacceptable behavior). These situations are difficult to manage because if the teacher addresses the "banging of the book" the student may escalate and if the teacher acknowledges following

Geoff Colvin

the direction to sit down, then there is the risk of providing tacit approval for banging the book on the desk.

Criterion Problems. This behavior, another form of limit testing, occurs when students perform at a standard clearly below the expected level (where the teacher knows that the student is capable of better performance). For example, the class is asked to complete a page of writing and Carl does half a page (Carl has demonstrated that he can complete a page with similar assignments). However, when the teacher mentions that he has only completed half a page he starts whining and complaining how hard it is. Further negative interactions are likely to ensue.

Rule Violation. Students will deliberately break a rule knowing that staff will respond and follow through. Once staff responds to the rule violation, there is likely to be further negative interactions. For example, students have been asked to line-up at the classroom door when recess is finished. This particular student stands at the side and the teacher reminds him to line-up at which point he starts complaining about other students and the interactions continue with the teacher.

Whining and Crying. This behavior typically prompts immediate teacher attention or assistance and in some cases may obtain a teacher response that displays irritation or frustration.

Avoidance and Escape. With these forms of behavior, students are seeking to avoid certain tasks or responsibilities. The behaviors can be very time-consuming for staff in terms of verifying the student's need. For example, Craig may be proclaiming that he is very sick and cannot do any more work. The teacher has to interrupt instruction to determine whether the student is sick or is trying to get out of the work. Even if the student gets the benefit of the doubt, the student still misses instruction. If the teacher does not give the student the benefit of the doubt, there may be further escalation of student behavior.

Noncompliance:
Student runs away.

Source: IRIS Media, Inc.

Threats and Intimidation. When a student with problem behavior threatens staff, there is the expectation that this staff person will be intimidated. However, if staff responds to this threat in any form that suggests a challenge, then it is highly likely that serious confrontation and perhaps unsafe behavior on the part of the student may occur. For example, when a teacher directs a student to complete an assignment either now or after school, the student replies quite angrily, "I know where you live." Such threats are a serious form of aggression and need to be addressed very carefully otherwise there is a high danger of the student exhibiting unsafe behavior.

Verbal Abuse. Similarly, when students use offensive or abusive language towards staff, there is a strong likelihood that staff will address the behavior immediately. Staff response to verbal abuse can set the stage for more serious behavior from the student.

Destruction of Property. When students deliberately damage or disfigure property, staff will take immediate action which may lead to further negative interactions.

Example of Phase Four, Acceleration. An illustration of *Acceleration* behavior is presented in Box 2.4.

Box 2.4: Illustration of Phase Four—*Acceleration*

Ginger came into class wearing a T-shirt that had a message on it, "F... Y...." Some of the students laughed and the teacher asked Ginger to come visit for a minute. At the side of the teacher's desk, away from the students, the teacher told Ginger that the shirt cannot be worn in school as it has a rude message. Ginger said that she didn't think it was rude and that her Dad gave it to her. The teacher became a little more serious then and said, "Ginger, what you wear at home is your family's business, but at school we have a dress code that prohibits rude messages from being displayed." Ginger said, "Well that's kinda dumb." The teacher said, "Ginger, that's the rule so please go to the restroom and turn it inside out." Ginger looked the teacher in the eyes and said quite firmly, "No way. You can't make me do that." The teacher then said, "You have a choice of following the direction or I will have to send you to the Office." Ginger said, "I don't care." The teacher followed through with the office referral and the principal was called in to assist with the situation.

In this example the interaction with the teacher began with the student wearing the offensive T-shirt to class. There was every chance that the student knew the T-shirt was a dress code violation and that the teacher would respond. In other words, the student expected a confrontation by wearing the T-shirt. Once the teacher responded to the student, the teacher was put in a position to follow through as the student became more defiant. The situation escalated to the extent that the principal had to be called in to manage the problem. In effect, wearing the T-shirt set the stage for further negative interactions between the teacher and the student.

Summary of Phase Four—Acceleration

Overall behavior is staff-engaging leading to further negative interactions.

Phase Five—Peak

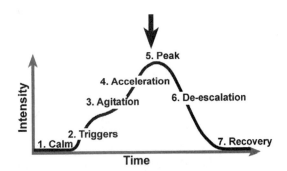

As the title suggests, this phase, *Peak*, represents the most serious or intense behaviors in the students' repertoires during the acting-out cycle. Generally, the students' behaviors are characterized by disruption so serious that class cannot continue or continues with difficulty. In addition, Peak behaviors often represent a threat to the safety of others or to the involved students. It is as if the student is in rage and out of control. These behaviors are often accompanied with hyperventilation and other body language indicating heightened anger and frustration. These Peak behaviors include:

Serious Destruction of Property. These behaviors involve substantial and costly damage to property. For example, the students may trash a classroom, throw a chair across the room or through the window, kick holes in the wall or push over bookshelves.

Physical Attacks. The student targets someone with the intent to cause physical harm such as punching, kicking, throwing objects, hair pulling, and even more serious behaviors including attacks with objects or weapons.

Self-Abuse. In this case the harmful behaviors are self-directed as in face slapping, hitting, pinching, hair pulling, head banging, and scratching.

Severe Tantrums. These behaviors include screaming, yelling, throwing objects around, pushing desks over, and flailing on the floor. While students are engaged in these tantrums, it is virtually impossible for the teacher to maintain instruction, that is the behaviors cause serious class disruption.

Running Away. In many cases, when students are out of control there is the choice of "fight or flight." Some students will elect to escape the situation

Peak Phase: Student threatens teacher.

Source: IRIS Media, Inc.

and run away. Their departure is generally accompanied with explosive behavior such as yelling, cursing, banging doors and kicking walls and furniture. These students can put themselves in precarious situations because their anger may impair their judgment, especially if they run away into dangerous areas such as busy traffic sections.

Example of Phase Five, Peak. An illustration of *Peak* behavior is presented in Box 2.5.

Box 2.5: Illustration of Phase Five—*Peak*

Carl has been arguing with the teacher for several minutes about whether he needs to do his share of cleaning up his area before he goes to recess. The teacher finally gave him an ultimatum that if he doesn't begin to help put things away he will have do his share during recess (Carl loves recess). At that point Carl became unglued. He kicked the chair and called the teacher several abusive names. He headed towards the door and pushed another student over who was in his way. He continued yelling and pounded on the door as he opened it and then ran down the hallway screaming, "I hate this … school!"

In this example the student did not get his way following his attempts with arguing and his behavior escalated. His basic behavior was to escape with a full range of accompanying acting-out behavior. It might be expected that if someone tried to stop him he would get very physical and perhaps cause bodily harm.

Summary of Phase Five—Peak

Overall behavior is out of control.

Geoff Colvin

Phase Six—De-escalation

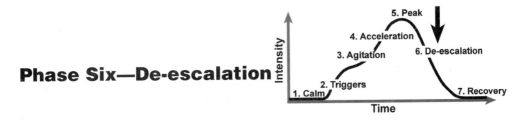

This *De-escalation* phase marks the beginning of the student's disengagement and corresponding reduction in intensity of behavior. However, the students are not especially cooperative or responsive to adult social influence. In effect the student is moving from a situation of conditioned or patterned behavior to one of more uncertainty and confusion. The phase is best characterized by calling it a *reintegration process*. The student is emerging from a period of very serious out-of-control behavior, *Peak*. The student behavior is similar to Phase Three, *Agitation*, where there is a very clear lack of focus and obvious appearances of distraction. The common behaviors manifested in this phase are:

Confusion. Immediately following a serious incident of being out of control, students will sometimes display confused, seemingly random behavior, such as wandering around the room, fidgeting, toying with items, staring at things momentarily, sitting, and standing. In effect, there appears to be a clear lack of focus in the student behavior.

Reconciliation. Some students will want to make up or test the waters to see if the teacher still likes them. They will offer to help or come close and stand near the teacher. Some may verbalize that they are sorry for what happened.

Withdrawal. Some students will put their heads down and try to sleep, either to withdraw from the situation or they may be genuinely fatigued following a prolonged acting-out period during Phase Five, *Peak*. In other cases, they need to simply quiet down to think things through and regain their composure.

Denial. Many students will engage in denial about their behavior especially regarding the most serious episodes during this acting-out cycle. Denial is very common when the students believe that they were victimized during the initial triggers.

Blaming Others. A common form of denial is to blame others. Students will frequently become quite animated and convey compelling conviction that the incident was caused by someone else. For example, the student may say, "It's all her fault. If she'd have let me see the nurse, this wouldn't have happened!" These students will avoid talking about the escalated serious behaviors and try very hard to hold the conversation around the triggers that caused the problems in the first place.

Responsiveness to Directions. Many supervisors have found that students will cooperate, almost willingly, to very concrete directions, such as, "Michael, please sit on the bench over there." It appears that the student is very distracted at this point and a clear, concrete direction provides a needed focus.

Responsiveness to Manipulative or Mechanical Tasks. Some students will become actively involved with tasks or activities that are very mechanical, such as sorting things, leafing through magazines or playing with toys, for example, Legos. These activities help the student become focused.

Avoidance of Discussion. At this point, most students will avoid discussion, debriefing, and opportunities to problem-solve. This author strongly believes that these discussions, while very important, need to be conducted later on in the next phase. The reason is that the student will not be open to problem solving and the discussion will center on denial and blaming others. The issue is timing.

Avoidance of Debriefing. Consistent with the students' reluctance to participate in class discussions and activities involving interactions, students will display avoidance behavior during any talk about the episode and their behavior or events leading up to the incident. For this reason debriefing should be conducted in Phase Seven, *Recovery*.

Example of Phase Six: De-escalation. An illustration of *De-escalation* behavior is presented in Box 2.6.

Box 2.6: Illustration of Phase Six—*De-escalation*

Jackson was out of control again, running around the room screaming and yelling, throwing things around, kicking over furniture and pushing other students. The teacher followed the school emergency procedures by sending the class to the library with an educational assistant and called for help at the Office. Once the class was removed and the principal arrived, Jackson started to calm down. He began to wander the room, and mumbled, "It's not fair. It's all her fault." He fingered the string on the blinds for a while staring out the window. He moved over to pick up a chair he had knocked over and looked sheepishly at the teacher. The principal directed him to sit in his own desk, which he did immediately. The principal told him that he was being very unsafe and could have hurt someone. Jackson pointed at the teacher and said, "She wouldn't let me finish my project and took it away from me." He then put his head down on the desk and refused to talk. The principal allowed him to sit for a while then said to him, "That's a lot better Jackson. O.K. now I want you to come to the office with me now." Jackson follows the principal and then the other students return to class.

In this example, the student was out of control and entered the De-escalation phase after the class left the room and the principal arrived. His behaviors showed signs of agitation and lack of focus. Moreover, in the initial conversation he blamed the teacher for the problem and then tried to withdraw by putting his head down. He then began to follow directions resulting in going to the office with the principal.

> **Summary of Phase Six—De-escalation**
> Overall behavior shows confusion and lack of focus.

Phase Seven—Recovery

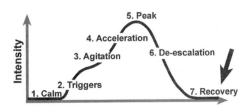

In this final phase, *Recovery,* the student returns to a nonagitated, and relatively normal state. Essentially, the student is able to participate, perhaps marginally, in instruction or the current classroom activities. The specific behavioral characteristics for this Recovery Phase are:

Eagerness for Independent Work or Activity. Typically, the students will become engaged in, or may actively seek, some kind of relatively independent "busy work." That is, activities that they have already mastered and require active responses such as coloring, looking up words in a dictionary and writing down the meanings, drawing, and writing. These activities need to be relatively easy and requiring little, if any, interaction with the teacher or other students.

Subdued Behavior in Group Work. While there is some interest in getting back on track, these students find activities that involve interactions with other students, or staff, very difficult. Strategies such as cooperative learning, or any activity involving working with others, would be very difficult for the student at this point.

Subdued Behavior in Class Discussions. Similarly, these students find it very difficult to contribute to class discussions at this stage. Also, when they are asked a question or are invited to comment, their responses are usually muted and cryptic.

Defensive Behavior. In this phase as they are recovering from a serious episode, some students will display behavior that is cautious and almost measured. They may be confused or wary or simply have learned over the years that it is best to be quiet at this time and say nothing.

Example of Phase Seven, Recovery. An illustration of this phase, *Recovery*, is presented in Box 2.7.

Box 2.7: Illustration of Phase Seven—*Recovery*

Jose was permitted to return to the classroom following an incident. He headed straight to his desk and pulled out his materials for the writing lesson. He began writing almost immediately. The teacher asked him if he knew what he had to do and he muttered, "I think so." He continued to write with a fairly high level of intensity. The teacher then announced to the class that it was time for them to get in their groups. Jose remained at his desk. The teacher encouraged him to join his group otherwise he won't know what to do. Jose joined the group but sat on the outside edge of the circle where his group was sitting. He didn't say anything and when one of the students asked him if he could do this part of the project, he shrugged. The group started on the project and Jose remained seated at the edge of the circle and began to look more closely at what his group was doing.

It is clear that this student was cooperating to a certain degree with teacher directions and responding to the group. However, it is evident that there was reluctance to say anything and he showed considerable caution in becoming involved with the group. While he was present in class and broadly following the class expectations, he was not really actively involved with the activities. However, it was evident that he was becoming progressively more involved with his group by watching the activities more closely.

Summary of Phase Seven—Recovery

Overall behavior shows an eagerness for busy work and reluctance to interact.

Summary Checklist of Phases in the Acting-Out Cycle

Appendix A: Form 2.1 provides an overview of the characteristic behaviors of each phase in the conceptual model of the acting-out cycle. The lists of behaviors for each phase are not meant to be exhaustive, rather, they are examples of the class of behaviors for that particular phase.

Appendix A

Form 2.1: Summary and Checklist for Acting-Out Behavior Cycle

Student Name: _____   Date: _____

Home Room Teacher: _____   Grade: _____

Phase One: CALM
Overall behavior is cooperative and acceptable

____ Maintains on-task behavior

____ Follows rules and expectations

____ Responsive to praise

____ Initiates appropriate behavior

____ Goal-oriented

____ Other _____

Phase Two: TRIGGERS
Overall behavior involves a series of unresolved problems

School-Based

____ Conflicts
    a. Denial of something needed
    b. Something negative is inflicted

____ Changes in routine

____ Peer provocations

____ Pressure

____ Ineffective problem solving

____ Facing errors in instruction

____ Facing correction procedures

____ Other

Nonschool-Based

____ High needs homes

____ Health problems

____ Nutrition needs

____ Inadequate sleep

____ Dual diagnoses

____ Substance abuse

____ Gangs and deviant peer groups

____ Compound triggers

____ Other

Phase Three: AGITATION
Overall behavior is unfocused and distracted

Increases in Behavior

____ Darting eyes

____ Busy hands

____ Moving in and out of groups

____ Off-task and on-task cycle

____ Other

Decreases in Behavior

____ Staring into space

____ Veiled eyes

____ Nonconversational language

____ Contained hands

____ Withdrawal from groups

____ Other

    Continued next page.

Phase Four: ACCELERATION
Overall behavior is staff-engaging leading to further negative interactions

___ Questioning and arguing

___ Noncompliance and defiance

___ Off-task behavior

___ Provocation of others

___ Compliance with accompanying inappropriate behavior

___ Criterion problems

___ Rule violation

___ Whining and crying

___ Avoidance and escape

___ Threats and intimidation

___ Verbal abuse

___ Destruction of property

___ Other

Phase Five: PEAK
Overall behavior is out of control

___ Serious destruction of property

___ Physical attacks

___ Self-abuse

___ Severe tantrums

___ Running away

___ Other

Phase Six: DE-ESCALATION
Overall behavior shows confusion and lack of focus

___ Confusion

___ Reconciliation

___ Withdrawal

___ Denial

___ Blaming others

___ Responsiveness to directions

___ Responsiveness to manipulative or mechanical tasks

___ Avoidance of discussion

___ Avoidance of debriefing

___ Other

Phase Seven: RECOVERY
Overall behavior shows an eagerness for busy work and a reluctance to interact

___ Eagerness for independent work or activity

___ Subdued behavior in group work

___ Subdued behavior in class discussions

___ Defensive behavior

___ Other

Adapted from: Walker, Colvin, & Ramsey, *1995.*

Geoff Colvin

Developing Behavior Support Plans for Acting-Out Behavior

The seven-phase conceptual model for the cycle of acting-out behavior allows us to develop a procedure for assessing student behavior and developing corresponding interventions. Form 2.2 (Appendix B) is a blank form providing a framework for developing an acting-out behavior support plan. This form is divided into two sections: *(a) Assessment,* in which the student's specific behaviors are identified for each of the seven phases in the acting-out cycle; and *(b) Strategies,* for managing each of the phases.

In order to develop a behavior support plan it is common practice to call a meeting involving all staff members who have direct responsibilities with the student. It is recommended that each of these staff members complete the Summary and Checklist for Acting-Out Behavior Cycle, Appendix A: Form 2.1, prior to the meeting. At the meeting, the chairperson secures consensus from the group on the key behavioral descriptors for each of the seven phases of the acting-out cycle and completes the assessment component of the behavior support plan, Appendix B: Form 2.2. In Section Two, corresponding strategies will be described for implementation at the onset of each of these identified behaviors. In Section Three, the strategies component will be identified for each phase to illustrate a complete behavior support plan.

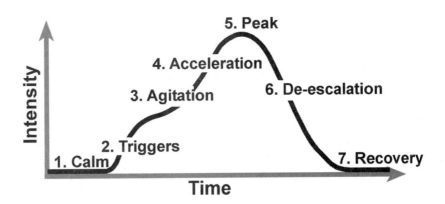

Appendix B

Form 2.2: Behavior Support Plan

Student Name:	Date:
Home Room Teacher:	Grade:
Staff Present:	

ASSESSMENT	STRATEGIES
Calm	Calm
Triggers	Triggers
Agitation	Agitation
Acceleration	Acceleration
Peak	Peak
De-escalation	De-escalation
Recovery	Recovery

Geoff Colvin

Case Study

At this point, we can examine a case study of an individual student to illustrate how Form 2.2 (Appendix B) can be utilized for developing a behavior support plan for a student who displays the cycle of serious acting-out behavior. In this particular school, the homeroom teacher for the involved student is required to write a summary description of the concerns. The completed summary is distributed to those staff who work directly with the student (Box 2.8). Each of these staff members completes the Summary and Checklist for Acting-Out Behavior Cycle, Form 2.1, prior to the meeting. At the meeting staff share their responses to the checklist form and the chairperson completes the assessment portion of the behavior support plan, Box 2.9. Please note that only the assessment part of the plan, left column, is presented in this chapter and that the strategies component, right column, will be added in Section Three, Box 11.1.

Box 2.8: Teacher Report for Behavior Support Plan

Student Name: **Kyle Jacobsen**   *Date:* **11/13/03**

Homeroom Teacher: **Walt Jones**   *Grade:* **5**th

In many respects, Kyle is a pleasant to have around. He takes pride in his work and likes to help. He has a few friends, not many though. However, there are times when he is very unsafe. When he loses it he storms around the room throwing things and has hit other students at times. I have had complaints from parents that they want him out of the classroom and don't understand why one student can ruin the education for others and make the room unsafe. It is very difficult to know what sets him off. Sometimes he is having a good day then he makes some errors and gets mad when you try to help him. Also, if any of my students try to help him he gets even madder. I think he feels inadequate and doesn't want to appear "stupid" to the other students. His parents are very concerned and they say he does the same things at home and has hit his younger brother a few times. They say they punish him by sending him to his room, not allowing him to use the computer, and taking away weekend privileges. But they believe that punishment doesn't make any difference. The parents think they need to put him on medication but they really don't want to. I would like to keep him in my class but I worry about the safety and disruptive aspects of his behavior. I am open to any suggestions and hope we can come up with a good plan at the meeting. Thank you for your time and support.

Signed: Walt Jones

Form 2.2: Behavior Support Plan

Student Name: *Kyle Jacobsen*	Date: *11/16/03*
Home Room Teacher: *Walt Jones*	Grade: *5th*

Staff Present: *Andrea Cole, Fred Carpenter, Wilson McCoy, Maieta Stephensen, Walt Jones*

ASSESSMENT	STRATEGIES
Calm *Likes to help* *Displays successful work* *Enjoys games* *Loves the computer*	Calm
Triggers *Repeating tasks* *Teasing remarks and put-downs from other students* *Facing corrections* *When he is given consequences for misbehavior*	Triggers
Agitation *Walks around the room* *Scowls at other students* *Pouts and mumbles to himself* *Does not concentrate on his work* *Complains about other students bothering him*	Agitation
Acceleration *Argues and will not quit* *Defiant and noncompliant "Make me"* *Name calls and threatens students* *Raises voice and shouts*	Acceleration
Peak *Throws objects around the room* *Kicks furniture* *Hits others students* *Threatens teacher* *Leaves room yelling and screaming*	Peak
De-escalation *Goes very quiet and puts head down* *If he leaves the room he hides and* * curls up in a corner somewhere* *Talks to himself negatively. "No one likes me." "I'm a loser."* *Likes to fiddle with things*	De-escalation
Recovery *Quite subdued* *Likes to work alone* *Looks depressed but tries to do some work* *Likes to draw*	Recovery

Adapted from: Walker, Colvin, & Ramsey, 1995.

Section One—Summary

In this section, a seven-phase model was presented for describing the cycle of serious acting-out behavior. Behavioral descriptions were selected from a large sample of students covering all ages from kindergarten through high school who exhibit this behavioral pattern. The primary purpose of classifying behavior in this way is to enable practitioners to understand the behavioral processes involved in escalating interactions between students and others (usually staff). The behavioral descriptions inform staff what problematic behavior to expect at each phase of the potentially explosive behavior chain. The overall expectation is that once the behavior pattern has been identified, staff is in a much stronger position to intervene early and interrupt the behavior pattern before it escalates into a serious disruptive and unsafe situation. The strategies or interventions corresponding to each of the seven phases in the acting-out cycle are presented in the following section, Section Two. In Section Three, a summary is provided and a complete behavior support plan is presented illustrating the specific assessment and strategies for each phase in the acting-out cycle.

Section Two—

Strategies

In the previous section, a conceptual model was presented for describing the seven phases of an acting-out behavioral cycle. In this section, information is provided on strategies that are designed to manage behavior in each of these phases. Since each phase represents a link in the behavioral chain, the basic approach is for staff to effectively manage the behaviors in the early phases. In this way the behavior chain may be *interrupted* thus *preempting* the later phases where the more serious behaviors occur. In the early phases one through four (calm, triggers, agitation and acceleration), emphasis is placed on teaching and prevention techniques. In the later phases five through seven (peak, de-escalation and recovery), the emphasis is on safety, crisis management, re-entry and follow-up procedures. These steps are depicted in Figure 3.1.

Figure 3.1: Strategies for Managing the Acting-Out Behavior Chain

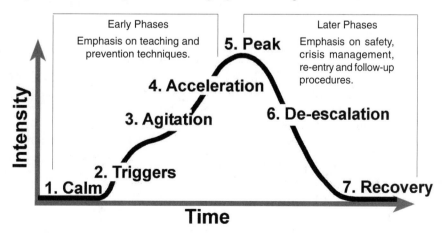

CHAPTER 3

PROACTIVE STRATEGIES FOR MAINTAINING CALM PHASE

The overriding goal in designing strategies for Phase One, *Calm*, is to keep the students productively engaged with instruction and learning in order to prevent any escalation of behavior. The basic assumption is that if the students are on task, challenged, achieving academically and successfully engaged in classroom activities, there will be less likelihood of serious behavior occurring. In this sense quality instruction is assumed to be a crucial preventive measure to controlling problem behavior (Colvin & Lazar, 1997; Sprague & Golly, 2004). Moreover, if a student has a serious incident, it is the classroom structure and instructional practices that will largely determine whether the student may maintain appropriate behavior once the incident has been de-escalated and the student returns to the classroom.

The purpose of this chapter is to describe five essential proactive classroom strategies for establishing a positive and structured environment that supports quality instruction and supports students with serious acting-out behavior. These strategies are: *(a)* Designing the physical space; *(b)* Developing a practical classroom schedule; *(c)* Establishing classroom expectations; *(d)* Implementing classroom routines; and *(e)* Managing instruction. The overall approach will be to highlight the central ideas of each strategy and present examples, checklists and recommended resources.

Designing the Physical Space of the Classroom

In today's classrooms many functions take place. Some activities occur on a regular basis while others occur infrequently. The success or failure of these activities in achieving their intended goals will, by and large, depend on the way in which the classroom is designed. Two steps are typically used to organize classroom space: *(a)* Clearly identify the full range of functions and activities that are likely to occur in the classroom; and *(b)* Carefully arrange the room in a way to ensure that each of these functions may be accomplished. Obviously the specific activities for each classroom will vary depending on the age group of the students and the subject matter to be taught. The following list of functions with guidelines for classroom design is relatively common to all classrooms.

Independent work location. This area requires minimum distractions. Areas for independent work should be in a low-traffic section away from materials and from time-out and free-time activity areas.

Group-work locations. These areas should ensure that students can easily attend to the teacher and to each other. A semicircle or row configuration of desks can facilitate group-oriented instruction.

Choice activities centers. Choice activities are sometimes used for students who finish their work early or as a reward for special achievement. Restrict this activity to a quiet location behind the instructional areas. Specific rules of behavior governing the use of these activities should be in effect.

Time out or penalty area. This area is used for students who need to be isolated in the classroom for displays of problem behavior. Select an area that isolates the student from the other students to limit their interactions This area could consist of a desk in the corner of the room, a small table facing the back of the room, or a desk at the side of the classroom.

Storage of materials and supplies. These are located in low-traffic areas to avoid distraction and yet allow easy access. Ensure that materials are neatly arranged and that they do not obstruct supervision or the students' view.

Teacher's desk. Desk is placed out of the path and flow of instruction. It should be located in an area that will safeguard personal property and confidential material.

Classroom seating by rows arrangement.   *Source:* IRIS Media, Inc.

Notice board location. The notice board should be highly visible in the room in a high-traffic area, but does not divert student attention during instruction. Divide the notice board into sections for specific communication, such as news, special projects and rules.

Obstructions to supervision. Maximize supervision by arranging the room so that all students are in sight. Be careful of high objects, such as bookshelves, that may obstruct supervision.

Quiet time area. This area is used to enable students to calm down when they experience stress or become agitated. This area needs to be as isolated as possible to prevent interactions with other students and staff.

Flexible seating arrangements. The seating arrangement can vary considerably. The key is *flexibility.* In developing a seating plan: *(a)* Ensure that all students can easily see presentations during whole-group instruction; *(b)* Minimize distractions; *(c)* Use clusters for group instruction; *(d)* Involve the students in the seating plans as appropriate; and *(e)* Vary the seating arrangement on a periodic basis (rows, semicircular arrangements, and clusters). Three examples of classroom and seating arrangements are presented in Figure 3.2.

Figure 3.2: Three examples of classroom and seating arrangements

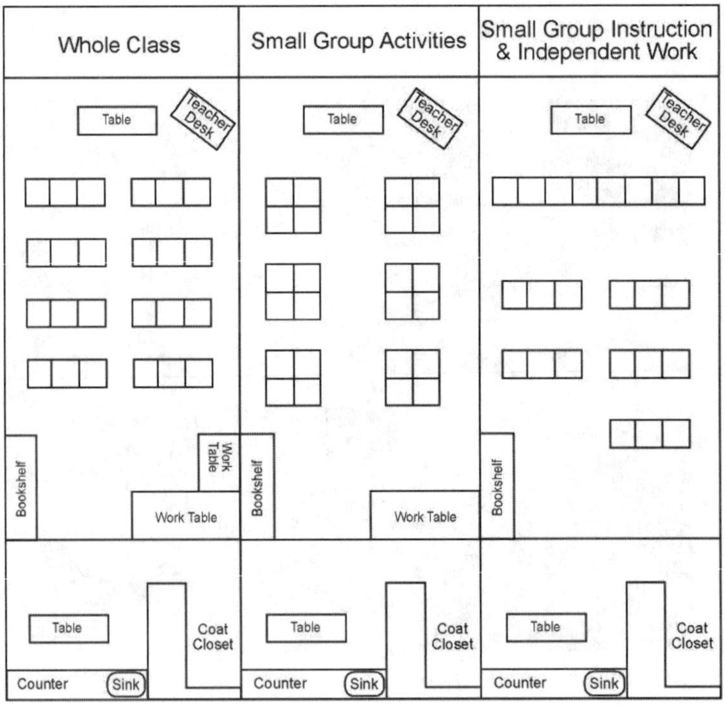

Source: Colvin & Lazar (1997), 6.

Classroom instruction and discipline are considerably enhanced when teachers pay careful attention to the multiple elements involved in the physical arrangement of their classrooms. Appendix C: Form 3.1 is a checklist designed for teachers to evaluate the design of the physical space in their classroom.

Appendix C

Form 3.1: Checklist for Evaluating Classroom Space

Activity	Completion Date	Notes
1. Locate specific classroom areas for:		_____
a. Independent work	___/___/___	_____
b. Group work	___/___/___	_____
c. Free activity	___/___/___	_____
d. Time out	___/___/___	_____
e. Materials storage	___/___/___	_____
f. Notice board	___/___/___	_____
g. Quiet area	___/___/___	_____
h. Other	___/___/___	
2. Draw up seating plans:		_____
a. Rows	___/___/___	_____
b. Clusters	___/___/___	_____
c. Semicircular	___/___/___	_____
d. Other	___/___/___	_____
3. Identify other classroom design tasks	___/___/___	_____
_____		_____
_____		_____
_____		_____
_____		_____

Source: Colvin & Lazar (1997), 108.

Establishing a Practical Schedule

One of the surest strategies for establishing a stable, predictable classroom environment for learning and for appropriate behavior is to develop a *practical schedule.* Cotton (1990), in an extensive review of research literature reported that schedules should be regarded as flexible time-management tools that are designed to best serve the educational needs of students. However, it is no easy task to develop a schedule since there are many blocks of time that have to be accommodated such as lunch time, recess, core subjects, elective subjects, specialists' periods, team teaching periods and district events. The classroom teacher needs to allow priority time at the start of the school year before the students return to develop a well-organized schedule.

Typically secondary teachers have little flexibility in developing a schedule in relation to the master schedule as the periods or blocks are determined by the master schedule based on subjects. Given that most secondary schools have adopted block scheduling involving 90- to 120-minute periods, teachers need to carefully manage their use of time within these blocks to maximize learning and minimize problem behavior.

In planning for a 60- to 90-minute block period the teacher needs to develop a schedule within this period of time. Canady and Rettig (1996) recommend that teachers utilize a variety of specific instructional activities and allocate a set amount of time for each activity.

The basic approach for elementary teachers is to develop a master schedule incorporating the fixed needs imposed by school-wide events (such as lunch and recess) and specialist teachers (e.g., art, music, and physical education). This master schedule is then adapted to meet the needs for first day, first week and first month of the school year. A checklist for developing a practical schedule is presented in Appendix D: Form 3.2.

Appendix D

Form 3.2: Checklist for Developing a Functional Schedule

Activity	Completion Date	Notes
1. Identify school-wide fixed schedules for:		_____
a. Start of school day	__/__/__	_____
b. Morning recess	__/__/__	_____
c. Lunch	__/__/__	_____
d. Afternoon recess	__/__/__	_____
e. End of school day	__/__/__	_____
f. Other	__/__/__	_____
2. Identify specialist schedule:		_____
a. Music	__/__/__	_____
b. Art	__/__/__	_____
c. Library	__/__/__	_____
d. Physical education	__/__/__	_____
e. Labs	__/__/__	_____
f. Other	__/__/__	_____
3. Identify team teaching periods	__/__/__	_____
4. Develop classroom schedule for:		_____
a. Master schedule	__/__/__	_____
b. First day	__/__/__	_____
c. First week	__/__/__	_____
d. First month	__/__/__	_____

Source: Colvin & Lazar (1997), 110.

Establishing Classroom Expectations

Perhaps one of the most undisputed beliefs regarding teaching and learning is the strong relationship between teacher expectations and student achievement and social behavior (Emmer, Evertson, Clements, & Worsham, 1994; Kauffman, Mostert, Trent, & Hallahan, 1998; Sprick, Garrison, & Howard 1998; Walker, Colvin, & Ramsey, 1995; Wong & Wong, 1991). Simply put, if the teacher expects the students to achieve and behave appropriately, they will. Conversely, if the teacher expects the students to achieve poorly and behave inappropriately, they will. Clearly, if these expectations are in place, then students who have problem behavior will have much more chance of behaving appropriately in this particular classroom.

Hofmeister and Lubke (1990) reported that the task of setting expectations is relatively easy since the majority of students know the rules in the first place. However, establishing the expectations is a more complex task that requires careful planning, long-term commitment and systematic implementation. In order to establish classroom expectations, the following steps are recommended: *(a)* Understand the function of teacher expectations; *(b)* Utilize best practice procedures for selecting expectations; and *(c)* Systematically teach the expectations.

Understand the Function of Teacher Expectations

Teachers must believe that their students can achieve high expectations in both academic skills and social behavior as a function of their instruction. However, an important discrimination needs to be made. There is a significant difference between high standards and high expectations (Kauffman et al., 1998). Standards refer to a group response, defining the level of achievement, academically and socially, for the majority of students. Expectations on the other hand, focus on individual progress. When a teacher sets high expectations, this means that every student is challenged to achieve academically and socially to their greatest potential.

Effective strategies for establishing behavioral expectations and for managing problem behavior emphasize directly teaching social behaviors (Colvin & Sugai, 1988; Darch & Kame'enui, 2004; Emmer et al., 1994; Sprick, Howard, Wise, Marcum & Haykin, 1998). Elementary teachers use a direct teaching plan involving five steps: *(a)* Explain; *(b)* Specify student behaviors; *(c)* Practice; *(d)* Monitor; and *(e)* Review (Colvin & Lazar, 1997). A blank lesson plan for teaching classroom expectations is presented in Form 3.3, Appendix E.

Here is a sample lesson plan, Box 3.1, based on Appendix E.

Box 3.1: Example of an Instruction Plan for Teaching Classroom Expectations
Appendix E

Form 3.3: An Instruction Plan for Teaching Classroom Expectations

---

Expected Behavior: *Cooperate with others*

Step One: **Explain**

There are many students in your classroom. All need to cooperate so that each can learn, belong and feel safe. Ask the students why it is necessary to cooperate with others. Ask them what happens when we cooperate with each other and what happens when we don't. Ask for some examples of cooperation and some examples which show lack of cooperation.

Step Two: **Specify Student Behaviors**

To cooperate means to:
1. Follow the teacher directions
2. Take a turn
3. Share
4. Work together when necessary
5. Follow the classroom and school rules.

Step Three: **Practice**

Use three steps to provide practice: (a) Individual model: The teacher models the behaviors, or select reliable students to model the behaviors, (b) Small group model: Select a few students to model the behaviors as a group and request the rest of the class to watch, and (c) Whole class practice: Conduct whole class responses. For example:
Individual model: The teacher says, "I am going to show you what following directions looks like. Joe will be given a direction followed by Sarah." The teacher asks Joe to take out his math book and open to page 54. Identify the critical responses such as, "Notice how Joe stopped what he was doing, got out his book and opened it to page 54 quickly and that was all he did." Present another direction to Sarah, "Sarah, put your books away and wait at the door please."
Small group model: The teacher says, "Now I am going to present some directions to Joe, Mary and Roberta. I want everyone to watch them." "Put your books away please. Take out your math book and open it to page 21." The teacher thanks the students for following the directions and the rest of the class for watching. Direct comments to whether the students followed the directions quickly. Repeat this routine with other students.
Whole class practice: The teacher says, "Now it is everybody's turn. Listen for the direction, follow the direction quickly and please do not do anything else." "Put all your materials in your desk and fold your arms on the desk please." Provide feedback and conduct a brief discussion on how the class did. Present additional directions for further practice.
Conduct practice sessions for the other behaviors related to cooperating, taking a turn, sharing, working together where necessary, and following classroom and school rules.

Step Four: **Monitor**

Now the students have an opportunity to demonstrate the expected behaviors during a natural setting. Monitor their performance by moving around and by looking around the classroom. For example, present the direction to remove their materials from the desk and get their math books out. Look around the whole classroom to observe students who have started to put their materials away and acknowledge them. For example, "I appreciate the students who have put their materials away already." Also, note the students who have not cooperated with the direction and prompt them. For example, "Some students have not started to put their materials away yet. Please hurry up."

Step Five: **Review**

Provide the students with feedback on how they performed with the expected behavior. For example if a high level of cooperation was obtained, "I am very pleased with the way the class cooperated with directions in this period. You followed the directions quickly. Thank you. Keep up the good work." If cooperation was not high, "We did not do very well with following directions this period. Some students did well. Thank you. But most of the class was too slow to follow the directions. I will remind you next period to try to be quicker. Let's see if we can improve."

Adapted from: Colvin & Lazar (1997), 17–18.

The main difference between teaching behavior to secondary students and elementary students is that there usually is less need for the practice step at the secondary level (Step Three, Box 3.1). The teaching plan for older students reduces to three steps, *(a)* Remind; *(b)* Supervise; and *(c)* Provide feedback. An example of an instructional plan to teach an expectation for secondary students is provided in Box 3.2.

Box 3.2: Example of Middle School Plan to Teach Coming to Class on Time

Remind

Explain to the students that we need to get to class on time so that we can use allocated time for instruction and learning. Moreover we need to be somewhat orderly in the hallways to help us get to class and to avoid disruption. Point out that it is OK to chat, but to get to class on time students are asked to: (a) Keep the noise down; (b) Use appropriate language; and (c) Keep moving. Provide these reminders just before the period ends and the students exit the classroom, especially before the most troublesome passing times. The expectations are also read out during the morning announcements on the address system.

Supervise

All staff is asked to position themselves near the doorway or even a little out in the hallway so that they can be seen by the students. Use prompts to keep the students moving as needed and use this opportunity to greet the students as they come to class.

Provide Feedback

Provide a brief discussion at the start of the period on how the students cooperated with the expectations (keep the noise down, use appropriate language and keep moving). Acknowledge the students who were on time for class and cooperated with the three expectations. Provide some indicators as to whether the class is doing better or worse each day and encourage those who have not, as yet, fully cooperated. Establish some positive and negative consequences for those who keep the rules and for those who do not, respectively, such as gaining or losing privileges. Report your results at the next faculty meeting. Results and progress are read out during the morning announcements once a week for a while.

Establishing Classroom Routines

The overall benefit to the teacher and students for having well established classroom routines is *instructional efficiency.* A list of the advantages for establishing classroom routines is presented in Box 3.3.

Box 3.3: Benefits from Establishing Classroom Routines

- *Develops self-management skills.* The more the students can do by themselves, the more likely they are to be responsible for their behavior both inside and outside the classroom.

- *Provides opportunities to practice skills.* Practice is necessary for students to acquire fluency in skills previously learned and currently taught.

- *Serves test or diagnostic purposes.* The students' performance on these examples provides the teacher with information on which students have mastered the skills and which students are still having problems. On further analysis of student responses the teacher may be able to diagnose error patterns and generate strategies to correct the problems.

- *Manages "administrivia" efficiently.* Many items related to school-wide and district organization such as attendance, lunch choices, and announcements, can be managed by the students through a classroom routine.

- *Minimizes disruptive interactions.* Classroom and independent routines help to provide a buffer against problem behavior for certain students by engaging them independent activities that minimize negative or disruptive interactions.

- *Helps create a shared ownership between the teacher and students.* The more students are called on to contribute to the planning and management of the classroom, the more they are likely to experience and express ownership.

- *Meeting special needs.* Sometimes students may have particular problems that are private. To meet these needs the teacher has taught the class to use a signal or key words so their needs may be addressed.

- *Provides structured opportunities for socialization.* Students who have poor social skills can be afforded a relatively safe opportunity to share a responsibility with another student and receive recognition and attention from peers and the teacher.

Adapted from: Colvin & Lazar (1997), 21-23.

Classroom routines refer to those activities or procedures that teachers employ for the day-to-day running of the classroom. It is expected that these routines are completed by students with minimum assistance from the teacher. Essentially, the goal is to have the students manage these tasks by themselves. The routines usually consist of a number of sequential behaviors to be managed independently by the students. For example, a teacher may expect the students to turn in completed assignments and products at a specific place in the room, return to their desk and begin another activity without prompting from the teacher.

Independent work time.

Source: IRIS Media, Inc.

Geoff Colvin

Teachers should give careful consideration to the routines they plan to adopt in the classroom. A checklist is provided in Appendix F: Form 3.4 in which common routines are presented. Once the routines have been selected, the teacher then proceeds to teach the routines using the same instructional steps to teach classroom expectations described above.

Appendix F

Form 3.4: List of Common Classroom Routines

___ Starting the day or the period
___ Entering the classroom
___ Working independently
___ Securing assistance
___ Organizing and managing assignments
___ Conducting tests and quizzes
___ Speaking in class
___ Sending work home
___ Moving around the classroom
___ Establishing class helpers
___ Obtaining supplies
___ Using the restroom
___ Using the water fountain
___ Meeting special needs
___ Using filler activities

Adapted from: Colvin & Lazar (1997), 21-23.

Managing Instruction

It has been well established that academic underachievement and problem behavior go hand-in-hand (Kaufman, 2001). The converse is also true. If students are actively and productively engaged with their learning, there will be less likelihood of behavior problems occurring. While there is considerable variability in the way teachers provide instruction, the following three instructional areas are considered to be crucial for students with problem behavior: *(a)* Assessment and curriculum planning; *(b)* Delivering instruction; and *(c)* Intervening during instruction.

Student Assessment and Curriculum Planning

Accurate student assessment in academic areas is particularly important for students who exhibit serious problem behavior. The first reason is that if these students placed in programs or content that they have already mastered, they are likely to become bored and disruptive. Moreover, some students may take offense when they are asked to do work that they can already do and may subsequently act-out. Secondly, if the assessment is inaccurate and these students are placed in content that is far beyond their skill level, they are very likely to become frustrated and will display problem behavior. Finally, considerable care needs to be taken in assessing the students. The reason is that students who display problem behavior, especially serious behavior, experience intermittent learning patterns. In practice, their behavior often keeps them out of the classroom or their behavior prevents them from performing the necessary practice to become fluent in the skills being taught. Consequently, they often possess "splinter skills." That is, the students manifest part of the skills but not all or exhibit the whole skill one time but not the next. Accurate assessment is necessary to determine the level of proficiency attained by these students.

Similarly, students can be left behind if the curriculum is poorly designed (Engelmann & Steely, 2004; Sprague & Golly, 2004). Colvin, Greenberg, and Sherman, 1993) reported several studies in which students with severe emotional problems made significant gains in academic performance, on-task behavior and overall desirable behavior through using Direct Instruction curricula. These curricula are highly structured and carefully designed to ensure students learn the targeted academic skills (Engelmann & Carnine, 1982; Engelmann & Steely, 2004).

In general, teachers should pay close attention to their choice of curriculum. They should ensure that the curriculum has a research basis for its development and implementation and that the teacher guidelines are sufficient for the teacher to implement the content reliably.

Delivering Instruction

In a well designed classroom, careful attention is given to the use of effective teaching strategies. These strategies increase instructional time and student learning. In addition, a strong relationship exists between effective teaching practices and positive student behavior. If all students are actively engaged in the lesson at hand, the chances of problem behavior occurring are greatly diminished. A checklist is provided in Appendix G: Form 3.5 for teachers to examine the instructional practices used in their classrooms.

Appendix G

Form 3.5: Checklist for Examining Instructional Practices

___ Instructional objectives specified

___ Teaching to mastery practiced

___ Continuous academic measures are employed

___ Instruction is geared to student success (approximately 75-80% success for new learning)

___ Students are successful at the rate of at least 90% for independent work

___ Students are engaged in on-task work quickly

___ Students are given opportunities to respond at a reasonable rate

___ Planned variation of instruction is used

___ Lesson activity flow is maintained

___ Academic learning time is maximized

___ Systematic error correction procedures are used

___ Student feedback on assignments turned in is reasonably quick

Intervening During Instruction

Teachers can maintain quality instruction and prevent a number of problem behaviors by paying careful attention to the strategies just described for delivering instruction. However, when students become off-task or are slow to become on-task, problem behavior will arise (especially for the student with acting-out behavior). A checklist is provided in Appendix H: Form 3.6 for teachers to examine a number of strategies that are successful in helping students to become on-task and for correcting students who may have become off-task, that is strategies for intervening during instruction.

Appendix H

Form 3.6: Checklist for Examining Strategies for Intervening During Instruction

___ Establish an entry activity and prompt students to engage quickly

___ Make initial explanations brief

___ Secure all students' attention before giving explanations

___ Plan for difficult transitions

___ Use direct speech

___ Avoid dead time

___ Settle students down at the end of the period

Chapter Summary

Students who display acting-out behavior often have periods where they are calm, can function adequately and can obtain a measure of success with their learning. A crucial strategy for assisting these students is to provide a classroom environment that nurtures this phase. Teachers who can create stable, positive and predictable classrooms with a strong focus on quality instruction and learning usually are more successful in serving students with problem behavior.

The purpose of this chapter was to describe key strategies for helping teachers maximize instruction and thereby increase the learning opportunities for all their students. These strategies centered on classroom design, practical schedules, establishing classroom expectations and routines and providing quality instruction. The strategies were called *proactive* because once they have been implemented effectively, students are more likely to remain in the Calm Phase and thereby pre-empt the cycle of acting-out behavior.

Teacher acknowledging class cooperation.

Source: IRIS Media, Inc.

Geoff Colvin

Chapter 4

Precorrection Strategies for Triggers Phase

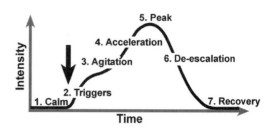

Strategies for the Triggers Phase

Students who exhibit acting-out behavior may function reasonably well in the classroom for several periods of time. However, certain events, called *triggers,* come into play and set the stage for problem behavior. These triggers, as we saw in Section One, may be specific events or a result of cumulative events. The triggers can occur at school or outside the school setting or some combination of both settings. Moreover, the triggers can be immediate events or events that have occurred earlier and were unsatisfactorily resolved for the student. Clearly, if the triggers are identified and effectively resolved, the student has more chance or returning to the calm phase and functioning at an acceptable level of behavior. However, if the triggers are not identified nor resolved, then it is only a matter of time before the student's behavior will escalate.

There are two basic steps in managing triggers: *(a)* Identify the triggers that set off problem behavior for the student; and *(b)* Develop strategies for managing the triggers, resolving the issues, and establishing appropriate behavioral responses. In Chapters 4 and 5, two levels of interventions are presented.

First Level Strategies. The first level, *Precorrection* strategies, is introduced in this chapter. These strategies target the context where the problem behavior predictably occurs. In this approach the triggers are *anticipated* and strategies are implemented *before* the problem behavior has a chance to occur. Overall, precorrection strategies are designed to manipulate the *context* in order to weaken the effect the triggers have in eliciting problem behavior. These strategies are relatively low impact in terms of classroom intrusion, especially teacher time.

Second Level Strategies. The second level of intervention, *teaching social skills,* will be introduced in Chapter 5. This intervention assumes the students do not have the prerequisite *social skills* to effectively handle situations that trigger problem behavior; or, that the students have learned unacceptable responses to certain contexts. The emphasis in this strategy is to provide formal social skills instruction, usually by means of a published or teacher-developed curriculum, to teach appropriate social responses to problematic situations. With more involved cases, it will be necessary to identify specific triggers, assist the student at an individual level with strategies for problem solving and provide family and community supports.

Managing Triggers with Precorrection

Precorrection is one of the simplest and perhaps the most effective strategy for managing triggers in school and classroom-based situations (Colvin, Sugai, & Patching, 1993; Kauffman et al., 1998). In many cases, teachers can identify the context or conditions when and where problem behavior may occur. For example, the teacher knows that at the end of recess, Johnny, Joe and Molly will be excited and hard to manage when they enter the classroom. Or, when students are required to work independently, Sara-Anne will become restless and engage in attention-seeking behaviors. Given this information, the teacher is in a position to act *beforehand* to address the problem behavior. For example, at the end of recess the teacher could meet the students at the door, have them line-up, come into class quietly and begin the activity written on the overhead. Or in the case of Sara-Anne, just before the students begin independent work, the teacher stands near her and helps her get started, moves away and comes back to her responding positively to Sara-Anne's on-task work. In each case the teacher anticipates problem behavior by identifying the setting and time when it is likely to occur and takes measures to foster the expected behavior before the students have an opportunity to misbehave.

The purpose of this chapter is to fully describe precorrection as a strategy for managing triggers that are likely to escalate students and to introduce measures that are designed to promote and establish acceptable behavior. The areas to be described are: *(a)* Precorrection as an instructional tool; *(b)* The distinction between correction and precorrection; *(c)* Critical precorrection steps and procedures; and *(d)* Precorrection checklist and plan.

Precorrection as an Instructional Tool

We saw in Chapter 3 that the fundamental approach for establishing classroom expectations and routines is to systematically utilize *instructional* procedures. Similarly, a basic assumption underpinning the use of precorrection strategies is that appropriate and inappropriate behaviors are learned. As such, specified behaviors can be taught applying the same principles that are basic to effective teaching of academic areas (Colvin & Lazar, 1997; Colvin & Sugai, 1988; Engelmann & Steely, 2004). This involves the systematic manipulation of teacher input (antecedents) and feedback (consequences) which, in turn, results in students learning the instructional objective. Precorrection procedures, combined with systematic correction procedures, parallel the techniques used for effective teaching in academic areas.

When students make an academic error, effective teachers utilize some form of systematic correction procedures. For example, feedback is given that there is an error, the correct response is modeled and then the student is given the opportunity to repeat the task independently. If students repeat the error on a frequent or predictable basis, teachers may introduce *precorrection* procedures such as prearranging the next instructional interaction so students are less likely to repeat the error and will have more opportunity to make a correct response. For example, if students are making errors pronouncing the "e" sound in a certain passage, the teacher may make a short list of common words containing this particular "e" sound and provide practice on these words *before* the passage is read. Similarly, if a passage contains some difficult words to pronounce or to understand, the teacher may go over these words with the class *before* the students begin the assigned work on the passage (Kame'enui & Simmons, 1990). These same academic procedures of correction and precorrection can be used to manage predictable social behavior problems in the school and classroom.

The Distinction Between Correction and Precorrection

To understand the parallel between the measures typically used to manage academic errors and social behavior problems, distinctions must be made between *correction* and *precorrection* procedures. In essence, correction procedures are *consequent manipulations* designed to stop inappropriate behavior *after* it occurs, while precorrection procedures are *antecedent manipulations* designed to *prevent* the occurrence of predictable problems and to facilitate correct responding (Colvin & Sugai, 1988).

Stetter (1995) reported in Kauffman (2001), a teacher of high at-risk second graders used precorrection procedures to teach her students to bring necessary items (utensils and napkins) when going through the cafeteria serving line. The students would frequently forget these items, return to the lines and cause minor disruption. The teacher focused on reminding the students to collect the necessary items *before* leaving the classroom and provided additional reminders when the students were entering the cafeteria line. The plan resulted in a dramatic drop in the number of students returning to the serving line and subsequent drop in minor disruptions. Stetter noted that in this particular instance, returning to the serving line may appear to be an insignificant problem compared to the kinds of problem behavior at-risk students may demonstrate. These seemingly minor behaviors, however, can lead to serious problem behavior very quickly, especially when staff addresses the initial problem behavior using direct correction procedures. In this case, however, the teacher manipulated the antecedents by providing reminders and effectively replaced the problem behavior with an acceptable behavior routine.

Precorrection Steps for Managing Predictable Behavior Problems

Precorrection procedures, used in conjunction with correction procedures, provide educators with a very effective and efficient method for managing a wide range of problem behavior that occurs in classroom and school settings. The combined use of these two procedures involve seven basic steps:

1. Identifying the context (trigger) and the predictable problem behavior
2. Specifying expected behaviors
3. Systematically modifying the context
4. Conducting behavior rehearsals
5. Providing strong reinforcement for occurrences of expected behavior
6. Prompting expected behaviors
7. Monitoring the plan

Pre-correction: Teacher provides two reminders.

Source: IRIS Media, Inc.

Geoff Colvin

Step One: Identifying the Context (trigger) and the Predictable Problem Behavior

The strategy of precorrection is based on the assumption that the problem behavior displayed by the student(s) occurs in a context that can be identified. In other words, the problem behavior is *predictable*. For example, a teacher reports that whenever the class is asked to work by themselves, Erika will become restless and begin to exhibit attention-getting behaviors such as talking out or whining, "This is too hard." Or, whenever the teacher wants to test the students on what they have learned, Jared will become ill and want to see the nurse or ask to go to the office to call his mom.

In effect, staff can often identify the *context* and the *predictable* problem behavior. The context can be any event, task condition, setting arrangement, circumstance, antecedent stimulus or trigger that sets the occasion for the problem behavior on some reliable basis. There are both informal and formal methods for identifying these contexts. Informal methods include simple observation, recall, records, and teacher notes. For example, a teacher may be asked, "Can you identify when the student is most likely to exhibit these behaviors?" In response, the teacher might say, "Well he is aggressive and disruptive a lot, but coming in from recess seems to be the most common time and that's when he is the most aggressive and disruptive." In this case the context is the transition from recess to class and the predictable problem behavior is aggression and disruption.

More in-depth information on triggers can be obtained by conducting functional assessments. This procedure is designed to systematically identify environmental variables that are *functionally* related to the student's behavior. These methods include direct observation, interviews, and systematic review of records. The goal of these procedures is to establish a testable hypothesis describing a functional relationship between a specific context and the problem behavior. Interventions are subsequently developed based on the hypothesis. More detail on these behavioral assessment procedures is presented in Chapter 5.

Step Two: Specifying Expected Behaviors

While removal of the student problem behavior may be a major priority for staff, the next step involves clearly specifying the behaviors we wish to establish with the student. The reason for this emphasis is that if we focus only on eliminating a problem behavior we may end up with other inappropriate behavior. We have a double objective: *(a)* To eliminate or significantly reduce the problem behavior; and, *(b)* Establish an expected behavior which serves to replace the problem behavior and set the stage for the student to be more successful in school. For example, if Charles talks out during independent work to get help, the expected behavior could be to raise his hand if he needs help. If a student consistently interrupts other students during discussions, the expected behavior might be to wait until someone is finished before speaking. In selecting the expected behavior, the following four guidelines are recommended:

1. Describe the expected behavior in *observable* terms. For example, "Raise your hand if you wish to speak."

2. Select behaviors that are *incompatible* with the problem behavior wherever possible (Engelmann & Colvin, 1983; Evans & Meyer, 1985; Horner & Billingsley, 1988). For example, "Go straight to your desk and start the assignment on the chalkboard." In this case the student would walk around the room disrupting other students. Thus, going straight to his desk and beginning work is incompatible with wandering the room and disrupting students.

3. Select expected behaviors that are *functional replacements* for the problem behavior (Carr & Durand, 1985). For example, a student may get teacher attention by talking out in class. The replacement behavior could be staying on task which secures teacher attention.

4. Select expected behaviors that are the *norm* in class. In other words behaviors exhibited by other students that are acceptable to staff. For example, students coming into class talk quietly to each other whereas Tanya talks very loudly. The expected behavior for Tanya when coming into class would be to speak quietly.

Step Three: Modifying the Context

The purpose of modifying the context is to increase the likelihood that the expected behaviors will occur and decrease the likelihood that problem behaviors will occur. In effect, when the context is modified the *stimulus control* for the predictable problem behavior is weakened thereby giving the expected behavior more opportunity to be displayed.

Numerous aspects of a given context can be altered, for example, the instructions, explanations, tasks, activities, scheduling, seating arrangements, reminders, and curriculum. For example, if Sally distracts Benedict, Sally could be moved to another seat. Or, if Alfred talks out a lot in a large group setting, he could be placed in a small group and taught how to take a turn.

Modifying the context is one of the essential and most effective components of a precorrection plan. The reason is that the modifications do not involve interactions with the student. The context itself is targeted for change.

Geoff Colvin

There are four guidelines for modifying the context:

1. *Modify the context beforehand.* Changes to the context need to be made *before* the student has an opportunity to respond (either appropriately or inappropriately).

2. *Minimize the changes.* The changes in the context should be as minimal and unobtrusive as possible. Change the context in minimal increments based on the occurrence of expected behavior exhibited by the student.

3. *Normalize the changes.* Ensure that the changes are as normal as possible. Try to avoid novelty, otherwise the changes in behavior may not maintain themselves.

4. *Systematically plan changes.* If substantial changes have to be made in the context to obtain expected behaviors, develop a plan to move from the modified or restricted context towards the normal or original context. For example, Billy may be required to play in a restricted area at recess. Once his behavior improves, the area he plays in can be expanded systematically until he is using the whole area for play.

Step Four: Conducting Behavior Rehearsals

There are two reasons why behavior rehearsals are necessary for an effective precorrection plan. First, once the student enters the target context, it is highly likely that the predictable problem behavior will occur. The problem behavior is under the stimulus control of this particular context even though the context may have been modified (Step Three). Second, behavior rehearsal or practice is a standard requirement for acquiring any new skill. Moreover, teachers want students to be *fluent* in exhibiting expected behaviors. Practice is the key to fluency (Colvin & Sugai, 1988; Engelmann & Carnine, 1982; Engelmann & Steely, 2004).

Essentially, this step involves presenting the student with some form of rehearsal *just before the student enters the target context.* The rehearsal may take several forms based on the student's age, time available and the severity of the predictable problem behavior. Common rehearsal forms include: reminders, reviews, having the student recall, re-state, read or demonstrate the expected behaviors. In some cases, with younger or more involved students, it will be necessary to conduct role-plays, model the expected behaviors and provide the student with several opportunities to demonstrate the desired behaviors. For example, Carlos frequently interrupts other students during group work. Just before group work, Carlos's teacher takes him aside with another student to conduct a simple role play and says, "Now in a few minutes we will be in our groups. Remember, it is very important to wait until someone finishes speaking before you say something. Carlos you watch me wait till Sylvia finishes talking before I talk." The teacher has Sylvia tell her about her morning and when she finishes says, "Thank you Sylvia, that was interesting." Now the teacher tells Carlos to be ready to ask a question once the teacher finishes talking. Carlos cooperates and the teacher says. "That's it Carlos and let's see you do that in the group, OK?"

Step Five: Providing Strong Reinforcement for Occurrences of Expected Behaviors

The major objective in the precorrection plan is to teach and establish specific expected behaviors in a setting that has previously set the occasion for predictable inappropriate behavior. Staff must realize that it is always difficult to replace an established behavior pattern with a new set of behaviors. In other words the new expected behavior will be in competition with the already established inappropriate behavior which has been reinforced intermittently over time (Horner & Billingsley, 1988). Therefore, to replace these behaviors, *strong reinforcement* must be provided for occurrences of the expected behaviors.

The kinds of reinforcers will vary from age to age and situation to situation. However, it is critical that *strong* reinforcers be used frequently in the beginning to offset the reinforcement history that has maintained the inappropriate behavior.

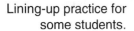
Lining-up practice for some students.

Source: IRIS Media, Inc.

Geoff Colvin

Step Six: Prompting Expected Behaviors

Even though the context has been modified to some extent and a behavior rehearsal has been conducted, the student may still exhibit the predictable inappropriate behavior. As indicated earlier, the inappropriate behavior has a reinforcement history, which increases the likelihood that the behavior will occur again. Moreover, the behavior rehearsals were conducted outside the target context. Consequently, once the student enters the target context, the *conditioned* inappropriate behaviors are likely to occur. Teachers need to be sensitive to the idea that the target context may *elicit* the predictable problem behavior. Students will actually need more assistance to exhibit the expected behaviors. The following four guidelines are designed as *prompts* for teachers to use when the student is in the target context:

1. *Use feedback praise.* Acknowledge the students immediately when they exhibit the expected behavior and use feedback in the praise. For example, if the expected behavior is to raise your hand if you wish to speak, then as soon as the student raises her hand to speak the teacher says, "Thank you Sarah for raising your hand. Now what do you have to say?" in a very pleasant and encouraging tone.

2. *Provide reminders in class directions.* When a direction is given in class, the teacher could include the expected behavior as part of the direction. For example, in a social studies class on capital cities, the teacher might say, "Who can put up their hand and tell me the capital city of New Zealand?"

3. *Use gestures to prompt expected behavior.* Sometimes the occurrence of the inappropriate behavior is almost immediate. In these cases the teacher might use gestures to prompt the expected behavior. Suppose, for example, that just as the social studies class commences, Sarah blurts out a question. The teacher could look at her and put a finger to her lips to signal not to talk out and immediately raise her hand to signal the expected behavior.

4. *Provide choices for repeated infractions.* If the student persists with the problem behavior, the teacher could present a warning with the expected behavior as one choice and a small consequence as the other choice. For example, Sarah continues to talk out after the teacher has used the prompts above (1 through 3). The teacher presents her with the choice, "Sarah, you are asked to raise your hand if you wish to speak or you will have to leave the group and make up the time during recess." The teacher would then follow through based on the student's choice.

Step Seven: Monitoring the Plan

As with most behavior intervention plans there are generally two parts to a monitoring or data collection plan. The first part is a checklist and plan that describes what the teacher will do regarding each of the seven steps in the precorrection plan. A sample of a precorrection checklist and plan is presented in Appendix I: Form 4.1.

Appendix I

Form 4.1: Precorrection Checklist and Plan

Student Name: Date:

Home Room Teacher: Grade:

_____ 1. Context

_____   Problem Behavior

_____ 2. Expected Behavior

_____ 3. Context Modification

_____ 4. Behavior Rehearsal

_____ 5. Strong Reinforcement

_____ 6. Prompts

_____ 7. Monitoring Plan

© Behavior Associates.   Permission to reproduce for personal use.

Geoff Colvin

The second component of monitoring the plan involves collecting performance data on the student, either occurrences of the problem behavior or occurrences of the expected behavior or both. The data taken should be as simple as possible so that the teacher is not overwhelmed by the task. Typically, data is taken on *frequency* or *duration* of the problem behavior or frequency and duration of the expected behavior. For high frequency events it is usually more practical to *take* sampling data for the more troublesome contexts. For example, if the student disrupts other students basically in all periods, then the teacher might take a ten-minute sample during independent work (when the student's disruption is most common).

Case Study

The complete seven-step, precorrection procedure is illustrated in an example involving Yuri, a third-grade student who comes in from recess shouting, laughing, and pushing other students. Every day the teacher spends a considerable amount of time trying to get him settled so she can hand out materials and explain the math class. It often takes 5-7 minutes to gain control of him and have the class engaged with the math activity. The teacher examined the situation closely and completed each section of the precorrection plan. The plan is described in Box 4.1.

For data management, the teacher could have taken frequency data on noises, loud talk, pushing other students, and time taken to begin work. She decided to measure the time taken to begin work as charting the other behaviors might be difficult with the whole class coming in at that time and the teacher was wanting Yuri to establish a new routine. Moreover, the teacher felt that if Yuri was focused on going to his desk and starting work he would not be thinking of roaming the classroom and interfering with other students. (Yuri would be establishing an incompatible behavior.) The baseline data showed a range of 5-7 minutes for the time it took Yuri to enter the classroom and begin work. A week after the precorrection plan was introduced, the time measure was averaging one minute which was the norm for the rest of the class (Sugai, Kame'enui, & Colvin, 1993).

Form 4.1: Precorrection Checklist and Plan

Student Name: *Yuri Krystom*	Date: *4/2/03*
Home Room Teacher: *Sarah Endow*	Grade: *3*

√   1. Context *Transition from recess to the classroom*

√   Problem Behavior *Shouting, laughing, pushing; downtime before he complies with directions and becomes on-task*

√   2. Expected Behavior *Enter room quietly, hands to self, go straight to desk and begin entry task on chalkboard*

√   3. Context Modification *Teacher meets students at door, has them wait a few seconds until everyone is in line, reminds them to go straight to their desks and begin the math puzzle that is on the chalkboard.*

√   4. Behavior Rehearsal *Teacher reminds Yuri just before recess to come into the room quietly, go to his desk and start the math activity and Yuri was asked to repeat the expectations.*

√   5. Strong Reinforcement *Yuri was told that if he could follow the rules coming into class after recess, the teacher would be very pleased and that he could earn some free time on the computer (one of his favorite choice activities).*

√   6. Prompts *The teacher meets the class at the door and gestures for everyone to be quiet and points to the math activity on the board. She catches Yuri and says, "Let's get started real quickly on the math puzzle."*

√   7. Monitoring Plan *The teacher uses her watch to measure how long it takes Yuri to reach his desk and begin work after he passes through the door.*

Chapter Summary

There are many triggers that set the occasion for inappropriate behavior which may readily escalate to serious acting-out behavior. Correction procedures that address the problem behavior after it has occurred are essentially reactive, that is, consequences are manipulated following the problem behavior. Unfortunately reactive techniques with most acting-out students are ineffective and often set the occasion for escalated behavior.

However, in the case of effective instruction in academic areas, teachers manipulate *both* antecedents and consequences with a strong emphasis on manipulating antecedents. Based on the assumption that academic skills and social behaviors are *learned* and need to be *taught,* strategies for managing social behavior problems should involve manipulation of both antecedents and consequences. Precorrection procedures emphasize manipulating antecedents, specifically the context where the problem behavior can be predicted, to establish behavior patterns. In this way, the problem behavior can be preempted and replaced with acceptable behavior.

Chapter 5

Teaching Social Skills for Managing Triggers Phase

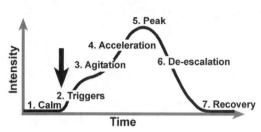

While Precorrection is an effective and efficient first level strategy for managing triggers that set off problem behaviors, some students may need more in- depth assistance and behavioral programming. These students are typically *very deficient in social skills.* The second level for managing triggers, Teaching Social Skills, will address the steps involving effective social skill instruction. Topics covered include: *(a)* The importance of social skill development; *(b)* Understanding the critical terms in social skill development; *(c)* Social skills assessment procedures; *(d)* Assumptions underlying social skills instruction; *(e)* Procedures for delivering social skills instruction; and *(f)* Intense individual programming.

The Importance of Social Skill Development

Social skill development, specifically the ability to relate appropriately with peers and adults, has long been considered a crucial aspect in students' development. Many authors contend that the ability to develop and maintain successful relationships and alleviate interpersonal situations is *predictive* of long term psychological, social adjustment and success in school (Gresham, Sugai & Horner, 2001; Kupersmidt, Coie, & Dodge, 1990; Sprague, Sugai & Walker, 1998; Sugai & Lewis, 1996; Walker, Colvin, & Ramsey, 1995). The truth is, social competence is considered to be essential for student success at school and in the community (Gresham, 2002). However, students who display serious acting-out behavior often experience significant problems in regard to social skills of relating effectively to peers and adults. One reason is that the peers are unsure of them. One day they can be quite friendly with their peers, while on another day certain events set the stage for them to act out and display hostile aggressive behavior towards their peers. These changes in moods and behavior cause peers to treat these students with caution and in many cases avoidance. Similarly, these students can be cooperative with teachers on a given day and yet on another day, when something goes wrong for them, they display belligerent and defiant behavior towards their teachers. Severe acting-out behavior can seriously jeopardize the normal development of social skills.

Showing beginnings of antisocial behavior.

Source: IRIS Media, Inc.

Serious acting-out behavior has been identified as one of the key indicators of antisocial behavior (Sprague et al., 1998; Walker et al., 1995; Kauffman, Mostert, Trent, & Hallahan, 1998). The prognosis for students with antisocial behavior is very bleak. In Box 5.1 a number of disturbing outcomes are presented for students who display antisocial behavior.

Box 5.1: Outcomes for Students Who Display Antisocial Behavior

√ Exclusion or removal to segregated settings is the most common response to students displaying serious acting-out and antisocial behavior

√ Serious acting-out and antisocial behavior is the primary reason for identifying students as emotionally disturbed

√ Severe aggression if not changed by Grade 3, is not likely to be changed

√ Children who grow up with serious acting-out and antisocial behavior are at risk for many long term problems such as dropping out of school, issues in the work force and substance abuse

√ Antisocial behavior is the most frequently cited reason for referral to mental health services

√ Students who display antisocial behavior are frequently referred for evaluation and special education services

√ Displays of serious antisocial behavior are the number one reason children and youth with disabilities are removed from school, work and home settings

√ These students are often classified as high-incidence disability groups

---

(Gresham, Sugai, & Horner, 2001; Sprague, Sugai, & Walker, 1998; Walker, Colvin, & Ramsey, 1995)

It is quite clear that students who display acting-out behavior to a marked degree either are deficient in social skills or at best are at high risk for being deficient in social skills. Given the importance of social competence for student success in school and the community, steps need to be taken to ensure adequate implementation of procedures designed to address this need.

Understanding the Critical Terms in Social Skill Development

Sugai and Lewis (1996) pointed out that there are literally dozens of definitions and descriptions of social skills and social competence. Moreover, there exists a wide range of subjectivity in interpreting social behavior. The following terms have been identified as crucial for understanding the purposes and directions of social skills instruction, especially for assessment and teaching.

Social Competence

Gresham (2002) defined social competence as "An evaluative term based on the judgments that a person has performed a social task competently" (406). The judgments are based on significant people (parents, teachers, community personnel, and peers) in comparison to some norm that is considered to be an acceptable criterion.

Social Skills

Social skills usually refer to the specific behavior exhibited in a particular context that meets social expectations or to perform competently in that context (Gresham, 2002). In this definition there is an emphasis on the *actions or behaviors* displayed by the students in a *specific context* resulting in a *social outcome.*

Social Skills Instruction

An educational approach is used in this chapter to describe social skills instruction. That is, the same principles and operations utilized for teaching academic skills are applied to teaching social skills. Using this model, Sugai and Lewis (1996) defined social skills instruction as, "Direct and planned instruction designed to teach specific social behavior that, when displayed by the student, results in positive judgments of social competence from peers and adults" (5).

Social Skills Assessment Procedures

In relation to problem behavior in general, the first purpose in social skills assessment is usually for screening purposes. That is, the procedures are designed to determine which students are in need of social skills instruction. For the purposes of this book, however, these students have already been identified. School personnel are already well aware that these students have serious problems, specifically in the area of acting-out behavior. The primary purpose of assessment for these students is to provide more detailed and particular information regarding their *social skills strengths and weaknesses,* and to provide direction for social skill programming and instruction (Gresham, 2002; Walker, Colvin, & Ramsey, 1995). Two approaches to conducting social skills assessment will be described: *(a)* Behavior rating scales; and *(b)* Direct observation.

Behavior Rating Scales

These measures are based on adults' knowledge of the student (usually the teachers'). Because of their knowledge of students at an individual level, teachers are excellent sources of information about the social skill needs of their students. Teachers are in an ideal position to not only identify target students in need of social skills training, but can provide reliable information on students who are unskilled, unpopular, socially withdrawn and antisocial in general. Behavior rating scales have been designed to tap knowledge of the student from teachers and other significant adults. These instruments elicit teacher judgments of students' social skills typically by using a Likert rating scale based on an estimated frequency of occurrence or severity.

A number of excellent social-skills rating scales are available for teachers. The *Buros Mental Measurements Yearbook,* available in any university library, is an outstanding source for evaluative information on the technical features of social-skills rating scales.

Some widely used scales include: *Social Skills Rating System* (SSRS) by Gresham and Elliott (1990); *Walker-McConnell Scale of Social Competence and School Adjustment,* (SSCSA) by Walker and McConnell (1993); and *Child Behavior Checklist and Social Skills Rating Scale* (Achenbach, 1991).

The overall value in the results of the behavior rating scales is that clusters of social skill needs can be identified. Some of the domains include: school adjustment, cooperation, assertion, peer relations, empathy, self-control, and responsibility (Walker, Colvin, & Ramsey, 1995). These domains allow for diagnosing and pinpointing the specific areas in which the student is having problems. This information can be used to effectively guide the content areas and curriculum choices for providing appropriate instruction to these students.

Direct Observation

Systematic direct observations provide critical information for social skills assessment. Behavior rating scales are somewhat limited because they are based on the professional's perceptions or impressions. By contrast, direct observations are conducted when the student is in the actual context enabling objective information to be gathered. There are a number of guidelines for conducting direct observations that help to ensure valid and reliable information is collected:

Keep the Process Simple. While a number of elaborate coding systems are available or can be created, recording procedures should be kept as simple as possible. In this way the observer is more likely to attend to critical information versus noting every possible behavior that may or may not be important.

Develop Precise Definitions for Behaviors Observed. At the onset of direct observations, every behavior that is recorded should be *operationally defined.* The definitions should be clear, unambiguous and complete. There should be no doubt in the observer's mind whether a targeted behavior has occurred or not. For example, it has been reported that Johnny displays negative social interactions with peers at recess. Negative social behavior was defined as:

> "The student is engaging in negative social behavior when he or she displays hostile behavior or body language towards peers; attempts to tease, bully or otherwise intimidate others; reacts with anger or rejection to the social bids of peers; or displays aggressive behavior with the intent to inflict harm or force the submission of peers."

> Walker, Colvin & Ramsey, *Antisocial Behavior in Schools,* (1995), 226.

Record the Dimensions of the Behavior. Social behavior can be recorded and measured according to several dimensions: *frequency* (how often the behavior occurs); *duration* (how long the behavior lasts); *rate* (how often the behavior occurs within a particular time frame); and *intensity* (a qualitative measure of the seriousness or gravity of the behavior).

Accurate measures of the dimensions of the behavior provide a basis for educators to objectively identify the social needs of the student, determine the level of urgency in addressing these needs and can serve as baseline measures to evaluate effectiveness of social skills interventions for these students.

Limit the Number of Behaviors to Observe. Some students may exhibit many problem behaviors. In these cases it is difficult to target all the behaviors of concern during an observation. Decisions need to be made to limit the number of behaviors to a manageable number for observation and subsequent social skill instruction. Three strategies for limiting the number of target behaviors are:

1. **Prioritize behaviors of concern and target the top three to five behaviors.** One way to prioritize the behaviors is to group them according to safety concerns, disruption and personal/social. For example, striking another student causing pain (safety issue) would be given more priority than talking out in class (disruption). Similarly, constant talking out in class (disruption) would be given higher priority over playing on a swing by oneself (personal/social).

   Note: Prioritizing behaviors means that these behaviors are targeted initially. Other behaviors not initially addressed would be targeted later on if they are still a concern.

2. **Target universal problem behaviors.** When a student exhibits many problem behaviors, sometimes it is helpful to target behaviors that are salient to most students who are antisocial or who act-out in a serious manner. Walker, Colvin and Ramsey (1995) suggest that these students spend more time *alone* and are *more negative* than their non-antisocial peers. Consequently, initial observations could target these two behaviors, being alone and negative interactions with peers.

3. **Develop clusters of behavior.** While a student may exhibit many behaviors of concern, some of these behaviors are related or belong to the same *response class*. For example, the response class of *social withdrawal* would include behaviors such as sulking, refusal to join in games, plays by oneself, walks away from peers, is frequently found alone. In this case, the particular response class becomes the target behavior and the observer would record the multiple examples under this behavior (Gresham, 2002).

Determine the Number of Observation Sessions. One of the major limitations of direct observations is that the target behaviors may not occur when the observer is present. For example, a teacher may exclaim, "Oh I wish you had come yesterday, then you would have seen it all!" Obviously the observer cannot be present at all times or even most times. For this reason careful consideration needs to be given to *sampling* the contexts where the target behaviors occur. In this way there is more chance that the measures are *representative* of the student's typical behavior for that setting. Generally three to five observational sessions are needed to sample to student's behavior for the specific setting.

Systematically refine the observations. It is important to understand that the initial target behaviors and coding system may need to be adjusted over time. Direct observation is a powerful and reliable measure. Once the data are collected it may be clear that the target behaviors need re-defining or that the dimensions for measurement are not sensitive enough. These adjustments need to be made in an on-going basis to provide the pinpoints needed for an accurate assessment and subsequent effective social skills programming.

Passing time with supervision.

Source: IRIS Media, Inc.

Assumptions Underlying Social Skills Instruction

In designing and implementing social skills instruction programs, there are a number of important assumptions. These assumptions help to define expectations and establish a rationale in programming for social skills instruction. In Box 5.2, some of the major assumptions are summarized.

Box 5.2: Major Assumptions in Developing and Implementing Social Skills Instructional Programs

1. *Social skills are learned behaviors that can be taught.* Sometimes this learning is unplanned (such as through watching others or viewing media programs), and sometimes it is planned (e.g., taught directly by parents or teachers), but in all cases children and youth have been and can be taught these skills.

Geoff Colvin

Box 5.2 Continued

2. *Behavior management problems are social skills problems.* When students misbehave in class by not following directions, disrupting others, displaying verbal and physical aggression, or bullying and harassment, we typically label these events as "behavior management problems."

3. *Social skills are prerequisites for academic and school success.* Social competence and academic success are highly correlated. Instructional activities involving sharing, cooperative learning, listening, and taking turns all require social competence. By contrast students who interrupt, do not share or cooperate, or do not listen are often excluded from the instructional activity and consequently do not achieve the learning outcomes for the lesson.

4. *The initial steps in setting up a social skills curriculum are time- and energy-consuming.* In order to become proficient in teaching social skills, teachers must commit the same time and effort needed for mastery of other curriculum areas such as math, music or writing.

5. *The ideal curriculum does not exist.* While there are many helpful social skills curricula available (see additional resources, page 81) no one curricula can be expected to cover the full range of contexts and problems that may be encountered in the various schools throughout the country. As with other curricula (e.g., math or science), teachers will need to adapt the content and activities to meet the needs of their particular students.

6. *The approach and components of social skills instruction are fundamentally the same as academic instruction.* The basic instructional design and practices required to teach social skills are functionally the same as those used to teach academic subjects. Even though the content differs (such as math content differs from science or music content), the curriculum design, practice examples, review practices, modeling techniques, assessment and correction procedures are common to all forms of instruction (Sugai & Lewis, 1996.)

7. *Social skills instruction alone may be ineffective with high risk or high needs students.* Some students, whose behavior is very serious and well established, may not respond effectively to social skills instruction. These students' behavior is too resistant for this level of intervention (Gresham, 2002). It is usually necessary to provide some kind of individualized program comprised of social skills instruction, functional assessment and perhaps wraparound services (Gresham, 2002; Gresham, Sugai, & Horner, 2001).

Delivering Social Skills Instruction

Once assessment information has been collected and the need for social skills instruction has been established, the next step is to formally teach the targeted social skills. The basic approach in delivering social skills instruction *is the same as* the principles and practices used in delivering academic instruction. Typically, teachers select a curriculum and then proceed to teach the curriculum following the same steps that are used in teaching from a math or language arts curriculum.

Selecting the Social Skills Curriculum

Given the variety and range of published social skills programs, teachers should use certain standards or questions for evaluating and selecting a particular curriculum. In Box 5.3 some critical questions have been listed.

Box 5.3: Critical Questions in Selecting a Social Skills Curriculum

1. Who is the target population of students?
2. What is the purpose of the curriculum?
3. What are the structural and administrative features of the curriculum?
4. What methods are used to teach social skills?
5. What instructional components are included in the curriculum?
6. Are assessment procedures included?
7. Can the curriculum be adapted for small groups and individual students?
8. What training is needed to implement the curriculum?
9. Is the cost reasonable and manageable?
10. Are strategies included to address generalization and maintenance of skills?
11. Have the procedures been piloted or tested and are the results available?

Sources: Engelmann & Steely, 2004; Engelmann & Carnine, 1982; Sugai & Lewis, 1995.

In general, whatever curriculum is adopted, teachers must adjust the content to the students' social skills needs based on previous assessment. In other words, teachers are encouraged to use the curriculum as a *resource* and make adjustments based on assessment and progress.

Recommended Social Skills Curricula

While several social skills curricula abound, the ones listed in Box 5.4 have been selected because they have been designed for students who exhibit serious acting-out behavior or fall into the category of more severe antisocial behavior. These programs emphasize anger management and control, resolution of social conflicts and social problems, problem solving and responsible decision making.

Box 5.4: Social-Skills Curricula for Serious Acting-Out Behavior and Severe Antisocial Behavior

Eggert, L. (2001). *Managing anger skills training (MAST).* Bloomington, IN: National Educational Service.

Goldstein, A., Glick, B., & Gibbs, J. (1998). *Aggression replacement training: A comprehensive intervention for aggressive youth.* Champaign, IL: Research Press.

Huggins, P. (1998). *Helping kids handle anger: Teaching self-control.* Longmont, CO: Sopris West.

Plake, B. S., Impara, J. C., & Spies, R. A. (Eds.). (2003) *The fifteenth mental measurements yearbook.* Lincoln, NE: Buros Institute of Mental Measurement, University of Nebraska.

Rhode, G., Jenson, W., & Reavis, H. K. (1992). *The tough kid book: Practical classroom management strategies.* Longmont, CO: Sopris West.

Schrumpf, F., Crawford, D., Usadel, H. (1991). *Peer mediation: Conflict resolution in schools.* Champaign, IL: Research Press.

Walker, H., Kavanagh, K., Stiller, B., Golly, A., Severson, H., & Feil, E. (1995). *First step to success.* Longmont, CO: Sopris West.

Intense Individual Programming

In Chapter 4 and the early part of Chapter 5 some well documented strategies were described for managing the Trigger Phase. However, some students may still exhibit serious acting-out behavior. In other words, these students need more intensive individualized assessment and behavioral programming. Two additional steps are frequently used to assist these students: *(a) Functional assessment;* and *(b) Wraparound process.* It is beyond the scope of this book to present detailed descriptions of these two valuable practices. However, a brief description will be provided followed by a list of important resources to enable the reader to pursue the topics as needed.

Functional Assessment

Very briefly, a functional assessment of behavior seeks to identify the functions of the behavior. Simply put, there are two broad functions or "causes" of behavior. First, to *obtain* something the student may find desirable such as attention, preferred activities, events or objects. For example, the student acts out in class and receives the teacher's attention immediately. The second function is to *avoid* something undesirable or aversive by running away, refusal to work resulting in removal, delaying tasks and escaping from responsibilities. For example, the student does not like reading, so when reading is scheduled she creates a scene resulting in removal from class (and reading). This information can be very valuable in understanding the purposes of the behavior and effective interventions can readily be designed. In general, interventions are set up to replace the problem behavior with acceptable behaviors that *have the same function.* If the function of the behavior is to obtain something desirable, student needs are met (access to something desirable); if the function of the behavior is *avoidance,* strategies are introduced to enable the student to be more successful in the context that the student finds *undesirable.*

Typically specific training is needed for educators to become proficient in not only conducting functional assessments, but also in using the information to develop effective behavior support plans. Over the past few years several excellent functional assessment guides have been published. In Box 5.5 some well known functional assessment resources are listed.

Box 5.5: Sources for Conducting Functional Assessments

Nelson, J. R., Roberts, M. L., & Smith, D. (1998). *Conducting functional behavioral assessment: A practical guide.* Longmont, CO: Sopris West.

O'Neill, R. E., Horner, R. H., Albin, R. W., Storey, K., Sprague, J., & Newton, J. S. (1997). *Functional assessment and program development for problem behavior: A practical handbook* (2nd ed.). Pacific Grove, CA: Brooks/Cole.

Sprague, J., Sugai, G., & Walker, H. (1998). Antisocial Behavior in Schools. In S. Watson & F. M. Gresham (Eds.), *Handbook of child behavior therapy*, 451-474. New York: Plenum Press.

Sugai, G. Horner, R. H., & Gresham, F. M. (2002). Behaviorally effective school environments. In M.Shinn, H. M. Walker, & M. Stoner (Eds.), *Interventions for academic and behavior problems II: Preventive and remedial approaches*, 315–350. Bethesda, MD: NASP Publications.

The Wraparound Process

In some cases, a student's level of agitation cannot be adequately addressed through a school program alone. One reason is that the triggers occur outside the school setting or the triggers are conjoint (occurring at school and outside the school setting). In these cases teachers often report that the student is "on edge" all the time, that is, the student never really settles down or that it takes very little to precipitate acting-out behavior.

Wraparound meeting: Parent, teacher, case-worker, kidsports representative, and student.

Source: IRIS Media, Inc.

When students do not respond to school-based interventions, another level of intervention can be utilized called *wraparound*. The wraparound process is a tool for building effective working relationships and support networks for students, their families, teachers and other service providers. Careful and systematic application of the wraparound process can increase the likelihood that appropriate supports and interventions are adopted, implemented, and sustained in all of the student's *environments* (school, home and community). This approach leads to improved student behavior in each of these environments (Burns, Schoenwald, Burchard, Faw, & Santos, 2000; Eber, 1997, 1999; Eber, Sugai, Smith, & Scott, 2002).

The wraparound process is defined as:

"A family-centered and strength-based philosophy of care to guide service planning for students with EBD (emotional and behavioral disorders) and their families. It involves all services and strategies necessary to meet the individual needs of students and their families. The child and family and their team of natural support and professional providers define the needs and collectively shape and create the supports, services, and interventions linked to agreed upon outcomes."

Eber et al. (2002), 172.

The planning steps for the wraparound process are listed in Box 5.6.

Box 5.6: Features of the Wraparound Process

1. Community-based
2. Individualized and strength-based
3. Culturally competent
4. Families as full and active partners
5. Flexible approach and funding
6. A balance of formal and informal community and family resources
7. Unconditional commitment
8. Development and implementation of an individualized service/support plan based on a community-neighborhood, interagency, collaborative process
9. Outcomes determined and measured through the team process

Source: Eber, Sugai, Smith, & Scott, 2002.

Additional resource: For a full description of the wraparound process see, Eber, L. (2003). *The Art and Science of Wraparound: Completing the continuum of schoolwide behavioral support.* Bloomington, Indiana: Forum on Education at Indiana University.

Wraparound process, an innovative approach for implementing individualized comprehensive services within a system of care, has emerged as a promising practice for improving outcomes for students who experience serious problem behaviors across environments. The effectiveness of wraparound, through the close collaboration between key personnel at school, family and service agencies has been well documented (Eber, et al., 2002; Malloy, Cheney, & Cormier, 1998; Stroul, 1993). Eber et al. (2002) provide a comprehensive description of the wraparound process and details for implementation.

Chapter Summary

Students who exhibit acting-out behavior are typically very deficient in social skills. Social skills are the tools by which students build and maintain quality interpersonal relationships. Moreover, these skills provide the basis for students to solve problems in a peaceful and constructive manner. The prognosis for students lacking these skills can be quite devastating for their success in school, behavior at home and in the community, and their future as adults.

Students lacking in social skills often exhibit problem behavior when certain situations arise, *triggers,* which can readily escalate to serious acting-out behavior. An obvious remedy is to provide social skills instruction to provide these necessary tools. The basic approach in teaching social skills is to use an instructional model that utilizes the same practices for teaching academic subjects. Essentially, if students lack the skills, then skills need to be systematically taught. Several well established social skills curricula are available to assist teachers in delivering social skills instruction.

In some cases, the student's behavior may be too serious to be changed through a curriculum approach. These students will require a more intensive individualized program involving functional assessment and the development of specific interventions based on this assessment. Additional support can be obtained by utilizing a wraparound process in which the significant student environments are targeted. A coordinated plan is developed involving school staff, parents and community agency personnel working closely in collaboration.

CHAPTER 6

CALMING STRATEGIES FOR MANAGING AGITATION PHASE

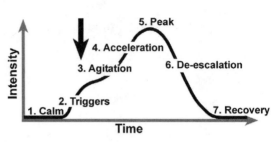

When students are exposed to triggers or the conflicts associated with them, it is only a matter of time before they exhibit agitated behavior. The reason is that they do not have the necessary skills to manage these triggers or solve the conflicts. The primary goal of managing behavior in this phase is to utilize strategies that are designed to help the student settle down and regain control. The alternative, as many teachers have experienced, is that the student may escalate to more serious acting-out behavior or remain at this level of agitation with heightened difficulty engaging in instruction. Clearly, neither of these alternatives are desirable.

These strategies are essentially accommodations involving slight departures from the normal procedures. The assumption is that the regular procedures may escalate the student or be ineffectual in addressing the agitation. Because the strategies are accommodations and supportive in nature, they must be implemented *before* the onset of serious acting-out behavior, otherwise, the chain of serious behavior may be reinforced. For example, Patty is off task and showing signs of agitation, shortly she begins to throw materials around the room, including a chair while cussing out the teacher. In this context if the teacher was supportive and exclaimed, "Oh Patty, I see you are agitated, would you like some quiet time?" This response would be inappropriate as the teacher would be providing a positive and supportive response to serious behavior. However, if the teacher responded earlier to the initial signs of agitation (grimacing, pencil tapping, slowness to get started), and used the supportive techniques, the student may gain composure and settle down to her work. The issue is *timing*. The techniques should be applied at the earliest indicators of agitation.

In this chapter, several strategies will be presented for addressing agitation that can be applied in a classroom or school setting. Finally, some limitations or problems with the procedures related to providing accommodations to students will be addressed.

Geoff Colvin

Strategies for Managing Agitation

Teacher Empathy

Perhaps the most powerful supportive strategy a teacher may use is to demonstrate *empathy*. To be effective, empathy involves two critical parts: *(a)* Understanding or recognizing that the student has a problem; and *(b)* Communicating concern to the student (Holm, 1997). For example, the teacher may see the student slouched in the chair staring at the floor (recognition) and then approaches the student and says, "Are you doing O.K.? Why don't you sit for a bit and I'll be back shortly (communicating concern)." Other similar empathetic comments include, "Do you think you can get through the period or do you need some time?"; "You don't look your usual self today"; and "You look a little stressed out today. Can I help you get started?"

It is very important to realize that the strategy of using empathy is much more effective if the teacher has already connected with the student. This connection or relationship has been established by the teacher taking steps to show interest in the student, respond to the student's interests and skill and give the student some time. In this way, when the student is agitated, he or she is much more likely to be responsive to the teacher's displays of empathy.

Assisting the Student to Focus on the Task

Students who display agitation often have difficulty focusing on their work, staying on task and concentrating. The reason is that they are essentially distracted by whatever it is that is disturbing them. Sometimes the teacher can assist the students to either get started or to resume their work. In this way the student's attention is shifted from the triggers that are bothering him or her to the specific activities of lesson. Thus by engaging in the lesson, the student's agitation is often reduced.

To help a student become engaged in a lesson the teacher may provide assistance by helping the student get started. For example, the teacher approaches a student who is just sitting, frowning and looking around the room and says, "Here Wianna, let me do the first one. There we go. Now let's see you do the next one." The teacher hands the pencil to Wianna, waits for her to continue and then says, "Nice going Wianna," when she starts to write.

Prompting on task:
Teacher helping student
get started.

Source: IRIS Media, Inc.

Providing Space

A very effective strategy for reducing agitation is for the teacher to provide some level of space or isolation from the rest of the class. The reason this intervention is powerful is because it is a strategy sought by the student. When students become agitated they will often seek ways to withdraw from others such as putting their head down on the desk, refusing to make eye contact or join in discussions, pulling away from the teacher or others when addressed, and heading to a corner of the room or a vacant desk. Their message basically is, "Leave me alone."

When students seek space, or are given space two outcomes are likely: (*a*) They are less likely to be provoked by other people or events; and (*b*) They are provided with an opportunity to settle down, regain a focus and become comfortable enough to resume the class activity.

Common strategies that teachers use to provide space or isolation within the classroom are to: establish a quiet area in the room to enable the student to retreat, such as a separate desk or a corner of the room; permit students to put their head down for a while; or allow them to move to an unoccupied desk or table. Sometimes it is helpful to lessen their involvement in the class activity. For example, one teacher told a student, "Byron, all you need to do is sit at your desk quietly. You don't need to say anything and I won't call on you."

Occasionally it may be appropriate to provide space outside of the classroom for more involved students, such as a supervised place near the office, a corner of another classroom, or a carrel in the library. In these

Geoff Colvin

situations arrangements with another staff person must be made ahead of time and provisions be made in case the student may escalate. The main disadvantage with providing space outside the classroom is that the student is clearly away from instruction and may have difficulty returning to class. Moreover, if a student does not like a particular subject, then this arrangement provides an opportunity for avoidance. In general, it is better to provide space within the classroom or the instructional setting.

It may be possible to designate some quiet area or space for the student to engage in relaxation activities. Teachers have reported that various kinds of relaxation exercises are helpful to reduce agitation. These activities include the use of audiotapes or CDs, breathing exercises, and relaxation exercises.

Providing Assurances and Additional Time

In general, students who display agitation on a frequent basis do not have effective problem solving skills, which of course is one of the reasons they become agitated. This situation is exacerbated when they are agitated. They often lack organization skills and the focus necessary to take charge of their responsibilities. Consequently, they may panic and exhibit worse behavior. In these situations it is often helpful to give the student some *assurances* and allow more *time* to deal with a task. For example, a teacher may say, "It's O.K. Maria, you have plenty of time to complete this." Or, "Take your time Marcus, you have several minutes yet before the bell rings."

Agitation Phase: Student, bottom right, left alone temporarily.

Source: IRIS Media, Inc.

In some cases, all the student needs is assurance at the onset of agitation. For example, Tia becomes agitated when she is cleaning up her space and the teacher says, "Take your time Tia, the bus will not leave without you." Or, "Tia, let me help you so you can get to lunch on time."

Permit Preferred Activities

When students exhibit agitation, they often have difficulty in focusing on a task. It is as if they are seriously distracted. One way of helping them become focused is to permit them to engage in a preferred activity. Because the activity is favored, it is likely to help the students disengage from what is bothering them and become connected with this activity. For example, Charlie, a first grade student often has trouble on the bus so when he enters the classroom he is already upset. The teacher has a desk in the corner of the room where he enters immediately and begins to play with some Legos. Or Ana, an eighth grade student who is frequently agitated when she comes to first period, is permitted to sit at the back of the room and read some magazines for a few minutes. Similarly, Josh has a hard time walking along the corridors at the High School. He believes that the students mock him behind his back so that when he enters the classroom he is grumbling over what the students are saying about him. The teacher has arranged that as soon as he enters the room, he heads to the computer and begins a game.

It is very important that the teacher set some parameters for the student when this strategy is used, otherwise the student may not leave the preferred activity or other students may interfere or want to participate. Generally, to offset or pre-correct for these problems the teacher needs to rehearse with the student(s) the ground rules for using these preferred activities. The rules usually include: *(a)* Only one person at a time can use the activity or occupy the area; *(b)* They are to use the activity individually, that is they are not to invite other students to participate; and *(c)* They are to use the activity for a specified time period with the expectation that when the time period has elapsed they move promptly to their assigned area or task.

It is also important to have more than one preferred activity available. The reason is that the student may become tired or bored with the one activity. Typically, the teacher learns which activities the student prefers either through observation or through conversation with the student.

Teacher Proximity

Often times when students become agitated, they become insecure. One reason could be that they have been there before and the outcome has been that they escalate and subsequently get into trouble. Or there is a level of discomfort for them when they are agitated. Consequently, when the teacher stands near the student during this period of agitation, the student may be reassured.

Proximity strategies include standing near the student's desk when speaking to the class, making incidental contact with the student, and initiating brief interactions with the student such as a comment or question, "How is it going there Bryan?", or "Looks like you have made a start there Jason." These contacts should be brief and if the student reacts a little, usually by body language, the teacher should withdraw slightly. In this case the student is communicating the need to be left alone.

Teachers may underestimate the importance of using proximity to assist a student who is agitated. It can be a powerful technique. The reason is that many students who act out do not have good adult role models in their lives, especially when they may be losing control of themselves. The teacher may be serving as their first appropriate role model. Consequently, when the teacher is present to the student during agitation, the student may experience acceptance at a time when the usual experience has been rejection or hostility. The overall outcome may be that the student becomes settled.

Agitation Phase:
Teacher using proximity
and encouragement.

Source: IRIS Media, Inc.

Independent Activities

One of the simplest strategies for leaving students alone, especially when they are agitated, is to schedule independent work opportunities. Independent work serves several instructional purposes such as opportunities for practice, mastery and skill assessment. In addition, this activity can provide a simple occasion for helping a student become settled and focused.

One of the most common reasons for students becoming agitated and accelerating their behavior is conflicts or negative interactions with their peers. Independent work, by definition, helps to factor out interactions between students. In effect there are fewer distractions giving the student more opportunity to focus on the instructional task.

In some cases, teachers have several students who display agitated behavior on a regular basis. In these cases, the teacher can schedule independent work activities on a regular basis. The schedule may be developed to involve some whole-class instruction, small-group activity followed by independent work. In effect, independent activities are planned to occur on a regular basis throughout the day.

Passive Activities

Similarly, following certain events such as recess, gym or assemblies, the whole class may be overly excited and some students may exhibit agitated behavior. In these cases, the teacher may utilize passive strategies. Passive activities require attention from the students but not much effort in terms of responses. For example, the teacher may read a high interest story to the students. The teacher reads the story and the students are expected to sit quietly and listen. A short video program can serve the same purpose. The students are expected to watch the video and sit quietly. Another example is quiet reading or writing a log given the students have the necessary reading or writing skills.

Movement Activities

It is often the case with adults that when they become agitated they begin to move, such as pacing up and down, moving to another area or getting busy doing something. However, in the classroom students are expected to sit still and relax or get on task with their work.

Movement is a tool that teachers can use to help a student who is agitated. Many students automatically show an increase in their behavioral levels when they are agitated. Consequently, when the teacher provides students with an opportunity to move, there is more chance that the students' needs will be met, helping them to become calm and focused.

An experienced teacher often has several movement oriented activities readily available, such as running an errand to the office, taking something to a nearby teacher, sorting materials, getting materials ready for another activity, cleaning the board or overheads, and distributing materials. In addition these tasks, or really jobs, set the stage for a positive interaction where the teacher may thank the student for helping in the classroom.

Student Self-Management Where Appropriate

Self-management is the ultimate, long term goal of any intervention program for problem behavior. Consequently, it is very important to actively involve students, where appropriate, in a plan to control agitation. Students often have their own strategies to reduce agitation and can contribute to the plan or program. For example, Micah had the practice of running away from the classroom when he became upset. When his teacher asked him why he ran away, his response was very telling, "I get into more trouble when I stay." So the teacher arranged with him that instead of running away from the school, he was permitted to go to a designated desk in the library. After some time of success with this strategy, the teacher was able to adapt the plan for him to go to a designated quiet place in the classroom.

In general there are two steps for involving students in the plan to manage agitation: *(a)* Help them to identify the onset of their agitation, that is to pinpoint when they first sense they are becoming upset; and *(b)* Arrange a strategy for them to follow when they recognize that they are becoming agitated. For example, Celia begins to shout and grimace when she becomes agitated. The teacher sat down with her and shared this observation with her and suggested that when she feels upset and thinks she might start shouting, she can go to the quiet area and sit for a while or play with the games there for a few minutes. In this way she is replacing the shouting behavior with going to the quiet area. A second example is presented in Box 6.1.

Once the student begins to work with the teacher to manage agitation, it is often possible and certainly desirable to arrange for the student to self-manage in other settings such as the cafeteria, recess or in other classes. In these cases the teacher would visit with the supervising staff and explain the arrangement. Some modifications may be necessary. For example, instead of going to a corner in the classroom to play games, the student may be permitted to move to a quieter area of the cafeteria. Similarly, the teacher would be encouraged to visit with the student's parent(s) and explore how the self-management plan may be implemented at home with parent support.

Box 6.1: Self-Management Plan for Roberto Entering the Classroom

Background: The teacher reported that as soon as Roberto, a first grade student, entered the classroom, she could tell what kind of day he was going to have. In other words his agitation was clearly observable and it was not very long before he was engaged in serious acting-out behavior.

Step 1: Recognize the Agitation

(a) Communication: The teacher visited with Roberto and said something like this, "Roberto, sometimes when you come into the classroom I can see you are really upset and it is not long before you are in trouble. Other times when you come in you look pretty happy and I know you will have a great day. We are going to work together to help you have a good day all the time."

(b) Signal: The teacher showed Roberto a card showing three faces, a happy face, an upset face and a "can't tell" face (where you cannot determine if he is *happy* or *upset*).

happy   can't tell   upset

(c) Application: The teacher then explains how the card applies to Roberto when he comes into class at the start of the day. Specifically the happy face means that he will have a good day; the upset face means that he will soon be in trouble, and the *can't tell* face means that he is not sure whether he is upset or not.

Step 2: Self-Manage

(a) Identification: When Roberto enters the classroom, the very first thing he has to do is to go to the teacher's desk, pick up the card, move to the teacher and touch one of the faces. The face he touches is based on his perception on whether he thinks he will have a good day, get into trouble soon or he cannot tell.

(b) Response: If he touches the *happy face* he goes to his desk and resumes the normal start of the day routine. If he touches the *unhappy face* he takes some quiet time (that is he goes to a desk in the corner of the room where he can play with Legos or other high interest games for about five minutes). Finally, if he touches the *can't tell* face he goes to the quiet area (fail-safe).

Box 6.1 Continued

Note: Suppose the student touches the *happy face* and it is very obvious to the teacher that he is upset. It is very important that the teacher allow him to follow the procedures and obviously keep an eye on him and intervene before he gets into serious trouble. If the teacher overrules him, then he will not learn to recognize his own state and will depend on the teacher. Moreover, the teacher would debrief with him later and point out that he touched the *happy face* and he looked very upset and was quickly in trouble. The teacher would then encourage him to be more careful tomorrow in which face he touches.

Two Possible Problems and Remedies

Because the strategies are essentially accommodations in an attempt to calm the student, two possible problems may arise: *(a)* The question of fairness to others; and *(b)* The likelihood of the procedures being used for avoidance purposes.

The Question of Fairness

While the teacher may perceive the strategies to reduce agitation as *accommodations,* the student's peers may perceive these strategies as *privileges.* Moreover, the peers may conclude that the privileges have not been earned. They witness the student having access to these privileges in the context of a recent acting-out episode. Peers may ask, "Why is … getting time on the computer and we have to sit here and do math? It's not fair." Or, peers may conclude that they have more chance of getting free time with games if they act-out rather than by doing a good job in the current activity.

The root of this problem of fairness is tied to the need to establish basic standards of behavior for everyone and at the same time, provide accommodations for troubled or needy students. The solution lies with the classroom expectations. Essentially, the teacher establishes *two* sets of expectations. The first set is presented as what is expected of everyone. These expectations are typically positive, proactive and functional, such as: do your best, respect one another, cooperate and take care of property. The second set of expectations is presented as exceptions. For example, the teacher may say to the class, "These are the expectations I have for everyone, 'Do your best. Cooperate. Show respect to each other and use school property the right way.' Now, sometimes I have to make exceptions because some of us need something different at times." In this way standards are established for the whole class and provisions can be made to accommodate individual students as needed.

Generally it is helpful to have a class discussion on why exceptions need to be made based on individual differences. These discussions help students accept that while they may need to be following the "expectations for everyone," one student may be given an accommodation. Furthermore, it is very important for the teacher to establish with the class that when exceptions are made, that the arrangement is between the student and the teacher. That is, the arrangement is not public knowledge so that the respect and dignity of the involved student is protected. This privacy component is best tied to the overall classroom expectations. For example, a teacher may say to the class,

> "I have two sets of expectations for the class. First, these are the expectations I expect for everyone, 'Do your best. Cooperate. Show respect ....' Second, sometimes I need to make exceptions because we are not all the same. However, when I make exceptions, that is between the student and me. I expect everyone else to stay out of it."

The Potential Issue of Task Avoidance

A second problem associated with providing accommodations to students with individual needs is avoidance. For example, the class is expected to do some expressive writing and this particular student, Monique, has challenging acting-out behavior and does not like expressive writing. The teacher has arranged with Monique that when she feels agitated she can go to the quiet area to have a little space and gain control of herself. So when expressive writing begins, Monique moves over to the quiet area where she is not expected to do expressive writing. In effect, she is using the accommodation strategy, access to the quiet area, as a way to avoid engaging in the task of expressive writing.

This problem is one that can be anticipated and the solution lies in how the program is set up initially. The recommendation is to design the program in terms of *two phases*. In phase 1 the student may use the accommodation freely. That is if the plan is to use the quiet area when agitation is present and there is no cost to the student. In phase 2, however, the student may use the accommodation but has to make up the time or catch up on the task that is missed. This plan is presented to the student as something to help the student become successful, but not something that is available forever. Essentially, the accommodation is presented as a *short term* intervention to help the student become settled. However, the expectation is that once the student begins to self-manage, the normal expectations for the class are followed.

Geoff Colvin

Chapter Summary

Managing agitation is a very important step in the overall plan for addressing serious acting-out behavior. In the first place, agitation often precedes serious problem behavior. If the teacher can successfully manage agitation, the student will become settled and not engage in the serious behavior. This interrupts the chain of behavior and serious acting-out behavior is prevented. Secondly, when students are agitated, they have difficulty engaging in their schoolwork. Basically, they are distracted. When the teacher uses strategies to settle down a student, the teacher thereby enables the student to participate in instruction.

A number of strategies were described in this chapter to facilitate reduction in agitation. Which strategy will work will be determined by the student. The teacher will need to try different strategies and carefully observe effects on student behavior. In this way the teacher will determine which strategies are effective for individual students.

Finally, while the strategies are designed to help students reduce their agitation, the teacher needs to pay close attention to how they are implemented. The reason is that the strategies are essentially accommodations which can lead to problems regarding issues of fairness with peers and possible avoidance behavior by the involved student. The problems can be precorrected by paying particular attention to the set-up details described in this chapter.

CHAPTER 7

DEFUSING STRATEGIES FOR MANAGING ACCELERATION PHASE

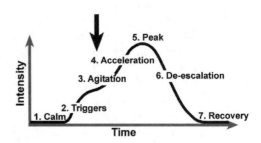

Last Opportunity to Avoid Peak Behavior

Effective management strategies are critically important during this phase in the cycle of acting-out behavior. If the behaviors are not managed successfully here, then the student is highly likely to exhibit serious acting-out peak behavior (Phase 5). In effect this is the last opportunity to prevent severe behavior and defuse the situation for this particular cycle (Colvin, 1999; Colvin 2001).

The basic defusing strategies are: *(a)* Studiously avoid escalating prompts; *(b)* Maintain calmness, respect and detachment; *(c)* Approach the student in a nonthreatening manner; *(d)* Utilize nonconfrontational limit-setting procedures; *(e)* Follow through; and *(f)* Debrief.

Studiously Avoid Escalating Prompts

Student behaviors during this phase are characterized as *engaging*. There is always the likelihood that some staff may directly respond to these behaviors in ways that may escalate the situation. For example, the student may be making rude noises and in response the teacher communicates disgust and anger and raises her voice to the student. The student then begins to shout back and throw things. In effect, the staff person has, probably inadvertently, escalated the student's behavior. Responses from staff that result in more serious behavior from the student are called *escalating prompts*.

The very first and most important step in managing accelerated behavior is for staff to *avoid* providing escalating prompts. The root problem is that the behaviors exhibited by the students may be taken *personally* by staff. Consequently, staff may react, become agitated, and resort to "in-your-face" kinds of behavior, such as finger pointing, that are highly likely to escalate the student. Unfortunately, staff often pay so much attention to the objectionable behavior exhibited by the student that they are not sufficiently aware of the impact their responses may have on the student and the connection to the subsequent serious acting-out behavior.

Moreover, accelerated behavior is designed to engage staff. Consequently, when staff reacts and exhibits agitation behavior, the student's initial engaging behavior is thereby reinforced. On the one hand, staff may believe that they are correcting the problem behavior, when in fact they are actually reinforcing it and setting the stage for more serious interactions. To lessen the chance of further escalation, staff needs to be very aware of the kinds of responses that are likely to worsen the situation and to deliberately avoid making them. These escalating prompts include:

- Agitated behavior from staff such as shouting
- Cornering the student
- Engaging in power struggles, for example the teacher retorts, "In my classroom you will..."
- Moving into the student's space such as leaning forward and pointing directly into the student's face
- Touching or grabbing the student
- Sudden or very quick responses
- Making statements that may discredit the student such as, "This is a high school not a pre-school"
- Becoming defensive and arguing
- Communicating anger and frustration through body language

In summary, the first steps towards defusing accelerated behavior from the student, or for preventing escalated behavior is for the staff member to avoid displaying any behavior that is *reactive*. These reactive behaviors are called escalating prompts because of the high likelihood that the students may, in turn, display more serious behavior leading to acting-out behavior.

Note: In the heat of the moment, a teacher may experience strong feelings of annoyance over a student's behavior, sensing that a negative reactive response may occur. In these situations, which are relatively common, it is best for the teacher to disengage from the situation, and return shortly. It is highly desirable to have a set response ready such as, "Just second, I'll be back shortly," then proceed to another activity such as moving to some on-task students to check their work or to acknowledge their on-task behavior. After a few seconds, the teacher having re-gained composure, returns to the student to address the specific behavior of concern.

Maintain Calmness, Respect and Detachment

While it is crucial to avoid escalating prompts, it is very important for staff to know what they should do in the face of accelerated behavior in this phase. The overall posturing for staff is to maintain a presence and posture of calmness, respect and detachment.

Calmness, is achieved by staff realizing that the student is "playing a game here," —that is, trying to engage staff. The most powerful response for staff is *no immediate response,* that is, to *pause.* The pause tells the student that his or her behavior is not getting to staff personally. When teachers can respond to the student's provocative behavior with a pause, the student gets the message that the teachers are in perfect control of themselves. In effect, the student's behavior is on extinction; it is not working in its customary manner.

Moreover, teachers generally agree that modeling behavior is a powerful tool for teaching and shaping desirable student behavior. In this scenario, the student exhibits inappropriate behavior designed to engage the teacher and experiences the teacher managing the problem in a calm and controlled manner. In other words, the offending student, along with other students in the class, see a first hand example of modeling how to address problem behavior. The teacher is serving as a good role model.

Another issue regarding calmness is the confusion related to the need to communicate to the student the gravity of the behavior. Basically, the student may exhibit behavior that is offensive to the teacher and the teacher wants to let the student know, in no uncertain terms, that this behavior is very unacceptable. However, in doing so the teacher may react in a way communicating anger which in turn may escalate the student to more serious acting-out behavior. The dilemma centers on how to communicate to the student that the behavior is quite unacceptable and at the same time avoid escalating the student. The solution lies in how the feedback is delivered to the student. There is less chance of escalating the student if the teacher can pause slightly and then in a *calm, measured* and *serious tone* inform the student that the behavior is very unacceptable and that some action would be taken.

Respect for the student's dignity and rights must be a critical consideration when teachers respond to problem behavior. *Any indication of disrespect will likely escalate the student to serious acting-out behavior.* A useful guideline for the teacher is to *focus on the student behavior,* versus focusing on the student. Careful choice of language can help in this regard, for example, the student uses expletives and the teacher responds, "That language is very unacceptable in this classroom," versus "Don't you dare talk to anyone like that."

Similarly, in addressing a problem the teacher can communicate respect by beginning with the student's name, for example, "Michael, that language is very unacceptable in class." By beginning with the student's name, the teacher is more likely to be respectful than if the teacher launches straight into the behavior.

Another respectful strategy is to speak to the student privately, such as taking the student aside. By emphasizing the privacy of the conversation, the teacher is also lessening the chance of the student having to "save face" in the presence of peers.

Detachment is a disposition that the teacher communicates to the student to indicate that the student is ultimately responsible for his or her behavior. In effect, the choice belongs to the student. While staff care about the student, it is very important not to communicate any degree of anxiety or any sense of coaxing and pleading for the student to behave appropriately. In this context, it is best to communicate in as matter-of-fact manner as possible and to make it very clear to the student that the inappropriate engaging behavior needs to cease or there will be consequences. The choice lies with the student.

Approach the Student in a Nonthreatening Manner

When students are approached in order to address the problem behavior in this phase, there is a high probability that the behavior will escalate. The teacher's behavior needs to be extremely controlled and nonthreatening. Some guidelines for approaching the student in this situation are as follows:

- *Move slowly and deliberately toward the problem situation.* Walk slowly, and avoid displaying behavior that indicates panic or anxiety. If possible, provide some on-task interactions with other students on the way to the target situation.

- *Speak privately.* Take students aside from their peers and talk quietly so as not to be heard by the peers. Avoid public statements and loud talk.

- *Speak calmly.* Use a flat, controlled voice. Be as matter-of-fact as possible and do not threaten.

- *Minimize body language.* Be as still as possible. Avoid pointing, staring at, or crowding the student.

- *Keep reasonable distance.* Do not get too close or invade the student's space. Avoid "Getting in the student's face."

- *Speak respectfully.* Avoid harsh, angry tones. Use the student's name, and speak in a soft, detached and respectful manner.

- *Establish eye-level position.* If students are sitting then sit beside them or squat beside them if possible. If students are standing, then stand. Some students react negatively to anyone towering over them in such situations.
- *Be brief.* Use language that is brief and simple. Long-winded statements or nagging will make some students react negatively.
- *Stay with the agenda.* Stay focused on the problem at hand. Do not get sidetracked. Deal with lesser problems later.
- *Avoid power struggles.* Stay focused on the problem at hand. Do not be drawn into, "I won't–you will," types of power struggle engagements.
- *Acknowledge cooperation.* In the event the students cooperate and disengage from the problem situation, be sure to compliment them on their decision. Also, mention their cooperation in a later report or follow-up to the situation.
- *Withdraw if the situation escalates.* Immediately terminate the discussion if the problem behavior escalates. Simply withdraw from the student and follow school emergency procedures.

The bottom line: Use common sense and approach the problem in a calm, detached, unhurried, respectful and step-by-step manner. Remember, the student's behavior in this phase is designed to engage the teacher. Consequently, the less the teacher becomes engaged or drawn into the problem, the more effective the teacher will be in defusing the situation.

Teacher responds quickly to student conflict in gym.

Source: IRIS Media, Inc.

Geoff Colvin

Utilize Nonconfrontational Limit-Setting Procedures

At this juncture, the teacher needs to have some strategies that are effective in arresting the student behavior. Essentially, the student's accelerated behavior has been challenging, off-task, defiant, noncompliant and overall engaging. The teacher has the double goal of needing the student to cease the problem behavior and resume the class activity. However, caution must be observed in *how* the teacher presents the direction or tries to establish some limits. For example, in a situation where the student has been wandering around the room for some time and not responding to teacher requests to sit down, the teacher says, "Listen here. You need to sit down right now and get on with your work or you'll stay in at recess!" There is a very good chance that the student will escalate and exhibit more serious acting-out behavior. The key to managing these situations, setting limits or presenting directions, *lies in the delivery of the directions.*

The following strategy is designed to provide clear and unambiguous communication to the student that the problem behavior needs to cease or there will be consequences and to present the information in a way that will not escalate the student. This strategy has three steps: *(a)* Establish initial setup; *(b)* Present the information as a decision; and *(c)* Follow through.

Step One: Establish Initial Setup

This strategy is more effective when attention is given to some details at the start of the school year. In this way there are no surprises for the students and the teachers do not have to think on their feet in the heat of the moment when the problem behavior may be accelerating. The two critical steps in setting up the procedures are to: *(a)* Rehearse the steps with the class; and *(b)* Establish a short list of negative consequences.

Rehearse the Steps with the Class. Early in the school year, preferably during the first week of class, the teacher should go over these procedures in the context of when other organizational items are explained. For an example of how a teacher may explain these steps refer to Box 7.1.

Box 7.1: Example of a Teacher Rehearsing Limit-Setting Procedures

Context: It is the first day of class and the teacher has just finished explaining the expectations in her classroom. The teacher had indicated that when the expectations are followed, good things happen (positive outcomes and reinforcers are listed. Similarly, when expectations are not followed, problems arise (negative outcomes and consequences are described). At this point the teacher explains what happens when students are too slow to cooperate or refuse to cooperate. Here is an example of a teacher's explanation:

"Now sometimes it happens, and I hope not very often, that some students will not cooperate, they are too slow to do what is asked or they refuse to do what they are asked to do. In these cases, you will be asked to do what is expected of you or there will be a negative consequence, like missing recess. Then I will give you a few seconds to decide. When I come back to you I will expect you to be doing what you are asked or there will be a consequence such as (you will have to miss recess)."

It is highly desirable to role-play this procedure so the students know exactly how it works. For example the teacher might say:

"OK, now let's see what it looks like. Michael would you stand over near the bulletin board and start looking at it? Now, I have told Michael a couple of times to go to his desk and start math. But Michael still stays reading the bulletin board. Watch me now."

The teacher approaches Michael and says:

"Michael, you are asked to go to your desk and begin work or you'll have to make up the time during free time. You have a few seconds to decide."

The teacher then leaves Michael, says something to the whole class about the schedule for the afternoon and returns to Michael. In the first role play he goes to his desk and begins work. The teacher thanks him and finishes the explanation of the schedule. In the second role play he does not go to his desk so he has to work during the next break.

Establish a Short List of Negative Consequences. The purpose of the negative consequences is to communicate the limits of behavior to the student. In other words, negative consequences will be delivered contingent on whether the student ceases to exhibit the engaging behaviors characteristic of this phase. The consequences, as with any consequences, need to be approved by school authorities and must be something that the teacher can implement. Note also that the consequence needs to match the severity of the student's behavior or potential behavior. For example, if a student is refusing to clean up before recess, the student may miss recess. Or, with more serious behavior, where a student is pushing a chair around the room and may engage in throwing chairs, the principal may be called. Typical consequences commonly used by teachers during this phase are:

- *Loss of privileges* (such as computer time, free time, free choice time)
- *Loss of recess or breaks*
- *Office referral*
- *Detention*
- *Loss of points*
- *Loss of something earned*
- *Parent call*
- *Time-Out*
- *Removal to another room*

Note: There is no "silver bullet" with consequences, that is, no one consequence can be expected to take care of the problem. *Mild consequences consistently delivered* is the key and is the most reliable rule regarding the power of consequences. For a more detailed description of the use of consequences refer to *The Effective Elementary Classroom* (Colvin and Lazar, 1997, 73-82).

Step Two: Present the Information as a Decision

The strategy in this phase of problem behavior, acceleration, is designed to prevent the student from engaging the teacher and thereby defuse the situation by putting the student's behavior on extinction. In effect, the student is trying to engage the teacher and the teacher will not become engaged. The intent is to *direct the focus* of the discussion or interaction to the expected behavior. The student is trying to engage the teacher through inappropriate behavior, however, the teacher does not respond in the way the student expects. Rather, the teacher focuses on the expected behavior and provides information that if the student elects to continue with the problem behavior, a negative consequence will be delivered.

It is helpful for the teacher to have a formula to use in this context comprised of three parts:

1. Present the *expected behavior* and the *negative consequence* as a decision for the student to make.
2. Allow some time for the student to decide (usually less than a minute).
3. Withdraw from the student, attend to other students or engage in some other task.

Examples of this strategy are presented for a kindergarten student, an upper elementary student and a high school student in Box 7.2, Box 7.3 and Box 7.4, respectively.

Box 7.2: Kindergarten Example for Limit-Setting

Context: The class is busy putting away their crayons, cleaning up and getting ready for recess. Ceta is playing with some Legos and has not put away her crayons nor cleaned up. The teacher stands not far from Ceta and acknowledges the class for their good efforts by saying, "I really like the way the class is putting their crayons away and doing such a nice job cleaning up. Thank you." Ceta continues to play with the Legos. A few seconds later, the teacher approaches Ceta and says,

"Ceta, listen to me please. It is time for you to put your crayons away and clean up *(expected behavior)* or you'll have to do it during recess *(negative consequence)*. You think about it *(decision)*."

The teacher moves to the closest students and praises them for cleaning up so well *(withdrawal)*.

Ceta hesitates then goes to her desk and begins to put away her crayons. Her teacher approaches her and says, "Thank you Ceta." Or, if Ceta did not go to her desk within a few seconds, the teacher would approach her and inform her that she is to stay in at recess and clean up.

Box 7.3: Upper Elementary Example for Limit-Setting

Context: Fifth grade students were working independently on a math assignment. Alex was out of his seat wandering along the side of the room and chatting to students who would listen to him or return the conversation. The teacher had complimented the class on starting quickly with their math assignment and for continuing to work. This compliment made no change in Alex's behavior. He continued to stand and chat to students. The teacher then approached Alex and provided a re-direction saying in a private manner: "Alex, look here, it really is time for you to be at your seat working. Please sit down and get started."

Alex gave the teacher a hard look and said boldly with arms folded, "Make me!"

The teacher prompted the students near Alex to keep working, "OK. Let's keep working here. Thank you."

The teacher then spoke to Alex quite softly but firmly, "Look Alex. This has gone far enough. You are asked to go to your desk and start work *(expected behavior)* or I'll have to send you to the office for defiance *(negative consequence)*. You have a few seconds to decide *(decision)*."

The teacher then turned and approached the nearest students, acknowledged their work and announced that they have a few minutes left to complete the assignment *(withdrawal)*.

The teacher returns to Alex after approximately 15 seconds and sees he is still standing there. The teacher then follows through with the office referral. Conversely, if Alex had returned to his desk and commenced work, the teacher would have briefly acknowledged him in a private manner.

Acceleration Phase: Teacher presents limit-setting procedure.

Source: IRIS Media, Inc.

Box 7.4: High School Example for Limit-Setting

Context: The class is working on a written history assignment except for Emily who has her head on her desk. The teacher moves around the class checking the students' progress and quietly praises the students' work. She approaches Emily and asks if she is OK. Emily lifts her head and puts her head down looking the other way from her teacher muttering, "I'm fine."

The teacher checks the work of the students near Emily then comes back to her and says, "Emily, it is time to get started on your assignment *(expected behavior)* or you'll have to do it in lunch detention *(negative consequence).* You have a moment or two to decide *(decision).*"

The teacher then continues to circulate around the room *(withdrawal).*

In a couple of minutes the teacher returns to Emily and acknowledges her if she has resumed her writing or follows through with detention if she has not resumed her writing.

Note: In these cases the teacher might take an extra step to ensure that the student is OK by using some of the strategies for managing agitation listed in Chapter 6.

Step Three: Follow-Through

The next steps taken by the teacher are dependent on whether the student decided to follow the expected behavior or to maintain the problem behavior. There are three common possibilities that the student may decide: *(a)* Exhibit the expected behavior; *(b)* Maintain the problem behavior; and *(c)* Maintain the problem behavior then switch to the expected behavior.

Student Exhibits Expected Behavior. If the student decides to exhibit the expected behavior, acknowledge the choice *briefly,* and continue with the lesson or activity. For example, the teacher would approach the student and say, "Good, you have joined the group, thank you," and move quickly to the other students. Return to the student shortly and interact briefly with the student on the task or activity and briefly praise the student's on-task behavior. For example, the teacher is checking the class's work, reaches the target student's desk and says, "Looks like you are getting it done. Nice job." Later, when the student is on task for some time, the teacher would conduct a short debriefing session (see Debriefing Session, page 110).

It is important to acknowledge the student's choice briefly and leave, that is move to the other students. The student may still be somewhat agitated and aggravated by a lengthy praise statement.

After the teacher acknowledges the choice, the student may make a low level negative statement. As mentioned earlier, it is best to ignore these responses and see them as face-saving remarks indicating that the student is still somewhat agitated. For example, suppose that the student is expected to sit down and get started on his math. The teacher acknowledges the student for getting started on his math and as the teacher moves away, the student mumbles, "I hate math." The teacher simply keeps walking and attends to other students.

Student Maintains Problem Behavior. If the students do not choose the expected behavior, that is they decide to maintain the present problem behavior, the teacher delivers the negative consequence. The language used by the teacher is important in order to communicate clearly. For example, the teacher may say, "John, you have not sat down (**expected behavior**) therefore you will have to do your work during recess, (**negative consequence**). Here the teacher informs the student of the penalty that will be delivered. A better way is to say, "John, you are telling me you have chosen to do your work during recess. OK that's what we will do." In this way, the teacher is clarifying the choice that the student has made. That is, the responsibility for missing recess in this case lies with the student. In effect, the student is accountable and responsible for the consequence that is delivered. Conduct a debriefing session later when the student has been on task for some time.

Student Maintains the Problem Behavior then Switches to the Expected Behavior. Once students become familiar with the teacher's follow-through procedure, it is common for them to try a delayed manipulation tactic. They will maintain the problem behavior and after the teacher tells them that they have chosen the negative consequence, they will then follow the expected behavior. For example, the teacher returns to the student and says, "John, you're telling me that you are choosing to do your work at recess. OK, that's what we will do." Shortly after, the student says, "Alright, I'll do my math now," and goes to his desk. Some teachers may be inclined to accept this delayed choice or "change of heart," and not follow through with the student having to miss recess. The problem with this response from the teacher is that the student may be learning how to stretch limits. That is, as long as he sits down at some point he will not have to miss recess. In other words, the student is testing the limits. The teacher really needs to *follow through* with the negative consequence in these situations in order to establish limits. It might be reasonable to have the student miss part of recess on the basis that the student did eventually begin work. Conduct a debriefing session after the student has been on task for some time and be sure to clarify that once the choice has been made, for example to work during recess, then the teacher will follow through with the choice.

Be sure to clarify with the students in the preteaching session that the moment for the decision will be when the teacher returns. If there is some doubt whether the student understands the decision process, give the student the benefit of the doubt and re-teach the procedures.

There are some additional points to be addressed or understood in relation to effective use of these procedures for setting limits and preventing escalation to serious acting-out behavior:

1. If students are displaying various forms of off-task behavior during this phase, it is very important to make sure that the student can actually do the work that is required. Clearly, if the student cannot do the work, then we might expect avoidance behavior and the real remedy for the problem behavior is more teaching or assistance with the instructional task.

2. Some students may exhibit reactive behavior when these procedures are followed. For example, when the teacher gives the student a few seconds to decide, and withdraws momentarily, the student may mumble or make facial expressions indicating disapproval. It is best to ignore these behaviors treating them as "face-saving attempts."

If the students escalate to serious acting-out behavior such as throwing a chair, yelling or uttering loud profanities, assume they are entering the next phase, Peak, and utilize the corresponding strategies presented in Chapter 8, Safe Management Strategies for Peak Phase.

Debriefing Session

The purpose of the debriefing session is to *problem solve* and prepare students so they will be better equipped to exhibit appropriate behavior the next time a problematic situation arises (Sugai & Colvin, 1997). There are four basic steps in the debriefing process: *(a)* Identify the sequence of events; *(b)* Pinpoint decision moments during the sequence of events; *(c)* Evaluate the decisions; and *(d)* Identify acceptable decision options for future situations.

Identify the Sequence of Events. Here the teacher walks the student through the series of events leading to the problem situation, during the problem situation, and following the incident(s). It is best to stay focused on the specific contexts and the actual behaviors exhibited by the student. An example of a student displaying noncompliant behavior and then following expected behavior is presented in Box 7.5.

Box 7.5: Example of Noncompliance and Delayed Compliance

Ana ended up in a situation where she overtly refused to do her work. Events leading to this refusal were the teacher told the class what math needed to be done independently and Ana stood up and began to walk around the room. The teacher eventually approached her and asked her to sit down and get started on her work. Ana refused, muttering, "No way." The teacher paused and told her that if she didn't start her work she would have to do it in her own time. Ana hesitated, frowned and then went to her desk and began her math work.

The teacher has taken the student aside and is visiting privately (or as privately as possible). The teacher helps the student identify the events leading to the problem. Specifically, the task was to be working independently on some math problems and the student was moving around the room. The teacher then goes on to identify the incident problem which was her refusal to start work on her math. The final event was the student making her way to her desk after too much time had elapsed.

Pinpoint Decision Moments During the Sequence of Events. This step involves helping the student see the relationship between decisions and subsequent events and to set the stage for making better decisions in the future. For the example above, the first decision the student made was to get up and walk around the room. Secondly, she refused to follow the teacher's direction. Finally, she chose to sit down at her desk and begin work versus doing it in her own time.

Evaluate the Decisions. This step is critical in helping the student understand that good decisions lead to positive results and poor decisions lead to more problems. The teacher helps the student evaluate each decision as good or poor based on the outcomes. In the example above, the decision to get up and walk around the room was a *poor* decision because she should have been at her desk working and the teacher had to come and give her a direction to start working. The student may object and say, "But I needed a pencil," or "But I can't do math anyway." In these cases, the teacher would point out that permission needs to be obtained for her to leave her desk or that the student could have raised her hand to get a pencil or to get assistance with the math. The second decision, to refuse to follow the teacher's direction, was a *poor* one because it resulted in the teacher having to give her a warning. Moreover, this decision was accompanied by saying, "No way," which is disrespectful. The third decision, of going to her desk and getting started was a *good* one because it resulted in getting back on track, avoiding having to do the math in her own time and obtaining a positive remark from the teacher regarding the choice. The teacher also pointed out to Ana that it was clear she did not want to do her work yet she still went ahead and began her work. The teacher told Ana that she had made a tough decision which was very pleasing.

Identify Acceptable Decision Options for Future Situations. The intent of this final step is to prepare the students for how they might handle future events differently so that incidents are prevented and expected behavior is more likely to occur. It is best to have the student actually commit to making *good* choices in the future and to rehearse the situation. A sequel to the example presented in Box 7.5 is described in Box 7.6.

Box 7.6: Sequel to Noncompliant incident (Box 7.5)

"Now Ana, when you are asked to do independent work next time, what will you do?" Ana is expected to say that she will get started on her work. The teacher might present some other needs such as, "Ana, what will you do if you haven't got materials such as a pencil?" or "What will you do if you need help?" Again Ana is expected to raise her hand, ask for help, and to stay in her seat. Finally, the teacher would say, "Ana, if it happens that I have to come to you and give you a specific direction, what will you do?" Ana is expected to respond that she will cooperate and follow the direction. The teacher would then strongly acknowledge Ana for cooperating so well with the debriefing session.

The debriefing session should be held once the student is back in the original setting, where possible. The reason is that the problem behavior emerged there, so the remedies should be addressed there, especially if it is the teacher who conducts the debriefing session.

It is also very important to conduct the debriefing session *after* the student is back on task. It is best to allow at least 10–15 minutes before the session is conducted to ensure that the debriefing session is a positive, problem-solving and supportive procedure that ends with the student having a firm plan for handling future events and with the teacher providing strong encouragement. When the students are back on task they are exhibiting cooperative behavior. The debriefing process assumes that the students will cooperate. Moreover, it is helpful to have some separation in time from the incident and consequences, if applicable, so the student will not associate the debriefing process with punishment or negative connotations.

Abbreviated Debriefing Process. In some cases, the teacher may not have time to sit down and conduct a debriefing process described above. In these cases, an abbreviated process is recommended. Essentially, the teacher asks three questions:

1. **What did you do that got you into trouble?**
2. **Why did you do it?**
3. **What could you do next time?**

For the example above the interaction would look something like this:

1. **What did you do that got you into trouble?**

   Student: I didn't follow the teacher's directions.

2. **Why did you do it?**

   Student: I didn't know how to do the math.

3. **What else could you have done?**

   Student: Put up my hand and ask for help.

Don't expect student responses to go as smoothly as the steps above. It usually takes some shaping and prompting by the teacher to obtain appropriate or accurate responses from the student.

Chapter Summary

Use of effective strategies in this phase, acceleration, is a critical step in managing the cycle of acting-out behavior. The reason is that the students can readily escalate to serious behavior or they can maintain this level of problem behavior which can be disruptive and very distractive in the classroom.

Teachers in general find this acceleration phase very challenging because the nature of the behaviors can be irritating and offensive. Consequently, teachers may react and subsequently escalate the situation. A major focus in the design of strategies for managing these behaviors is to pay particular attention to the way teachers may respond. The situation may be defused or escalated depending on the teacher's response. In general, the strategies used require the teacher to respond in a calm, planned, respectful and detached manner.

A second emphasis in the procedures is for the teacher to present information to the student in a way that puts the responsibility on the student. This procedure helps to factor out confrontational issues and at the same time puts responsibility where it belongs– with the student.

Finally, there is an emphasis on follow through and debriefing. The follow through gives the students feedback on their choices. Debriefing is designed to assist the students in understanding the pattern of events leading to the problem behavior and helps the students prepare themselves for future situations that may be similar.

CHAPTER 8

SAFE MANAGEMENT STRATEGIES FOR PEAK PHASE

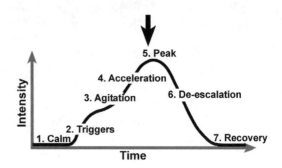

When teachers refer to acting-out behavior, particularly at a severe level, they typically mean behaviors that occur in the peak phase (Phase 5 of this model). These behaviors are serious, disruptive, and can often threaten the safety of others. If these behaviors are not managed effectively, the classroom is disrupted and the safety of others can be affected. In such cases, the logical or common step is to remove the student. However, if staff has to use force to remove the student, then the situation can become very serious where physical hurt may occur to the student or others, serious disruption is likely to occur and substantial damage to property may occur. In other words, the situation can become very dangerous.

The recent spate of tragic school shootings and other acts of school violence have given very strong impetus to the need for all schools to establish effective and efficient school emergency procedures. No school can claim with certainty that it is safe, nor can any school say, "It can't happen here," in reference to acts of violence. Many state education departments and school districts have responded by mandating and developing comprehensive school emergency procedures (Paine & Sprague, 2000; Sprague, Colvin, Irvin, & Stieber, 1997). There are many other dangerous situations that require prompt and efficient responses from school authorities, such as a gas leak, drug deals on campus, natural disasters such as earthquakes, and strangers on the playground.

Since acting-out behavior can involve safety concerns as well as serious disruption, the approach for managing the peak phase of acting-out behavior is to incorporate the procedures into the school policies and procedures, or district plans for managing emergency situations. Emergency procedures typically are designed around a number of critical components. It is expected that there will be variability within these components as a function of resources, age group of students and school locations. However, it is assumed that these essential components should be common to all plans. These critical components of a school emergency plan are: *(a)* Clear school or district policy; *(b)* Identification of possible emergency situations; *(c)* Guiding principles in

Geoff Colvin

dealing with safety issues; *(d)* Necessary prerequisites; *(e)* Action response plan; and *(f)* Follow-up.

Clear School or District Policy

All schools or districts should have a clearly written policy regarding school safety. The intent of this policy is to ensure the safety of all students and staff and that in the event of situations that may pose a threat to safety, appropriate measures will be taken.

It is, however, imperative that this policy is *consistent* with the stated educational vision of the school. For example, a district may have a vision to serve all students and a goal to increase its capacity to provide an appropriate education for each student. Yet the school safety policy may state that there will be no tolerance of behavior that threatens the safety of students and staff. This could mean that students who exhibit unsafe behavior are expelled resulting in exclusion from an appropriate education. In other words, the school policy on safety is *not consistent* with the school's educational vision. In this case the school safety policy could state that every step will be taken to ensure the safety of all students and to meet the educational needs of all students in an appropriate manner.

The school safety policy needs to be clearly written in positive terms with an emphasis on creating the kind of environment conducive to supporting learning, individual rights and safety for all concerned. This policy should be reviewed periodically and disseminated systematically.

Identification of Possible Emergency Situations

Once the school safety policy has been written and systematically disseminated, the next step is to specify the situations that may warrant emergency procedures. These situations could be identified by examining school records or school history, situations that have occurred in other schools that are similar in demographics— especially locations, information derived from surveys, and results from instruments that are available to determine the risk factors for a given school (Dwyer, Osher, & Warger, 1998; Stephens, 1995; Watson, Poda, Miller, Rice, & West, 1990). Situations that schools typically regard as emergency situations are presented in Box 8.1.

Box 8.1: Situations Warranting Emergency Procedures

- Strangers in the building or on the school grounds
- Bomb threats or explosions
- Students in possession of a weapon
- Serious injury or death
- Serious fight
- Breakdowns in the physical plant such as a gas leak
- Drug deals on campus
- Students in unsafe situations such as on the roof of the school building
- Natural disasters such as hurricanes or earthquakes
- Kidnapping or hostage-taking
- Student or staff exhibiting serious out-of-control behavior
- Student or staff under the influence of controlled substances exhibiting significantly unusual behavior

Guiding Principles in Dealing with Safety Issues

While emergency procedures require swift, efficient and effective action, there are a number of key assumptions underlying the procedures that need to be understood (Sugai & Colvin, 1999). The reason for these guiding principles is to ensure that the emergency procedures are in compliance with the educational vision of the school and the rights of all parties concerned in the incident. These assumptions include:

1. *Safety is the number one consideration.* Student and staff safety take clear precedence over other school needs. Other issues, such as whether the school is disrupted, are secondary. The entire school population must immediately cease what they are doing and follow the school emergency procedures to ensure safety for all concerned. Moreover, learning opportunities or teachable moments also are secondary considerations and must not get in the way of initial emergency responses. Secondary concerns are addressed in the follow-up procedures at the end of this chapter.

2. *Escalations are likely to run their course.* Some emergency situations involve serious escalated behavior, such as fights, severe altercations and disputes. These escalations will typically run their course. Provision needs to be made to allow involved persons to calm down and collect themselves.

3. *Follow-up and debriefing.* Once immediate safety issues have been taken care of, there is a critical need to follow-up, debrief and review the incident particularly in relation to how events escalated to the point of an emergency situation. In this way the patterns can be better understood and plans can be made to prevent similar incidents in the future.

4. *Tracking.* Complete records need to be kept of all incidents where emergency procedures have been used. These records are not only necessary documents for follow-up but also serve to provide information for the staff to make decisions regarding future planning. For example, the records indicate that a school has experienced more that a normal rate of incidents of fights. The school should then develop a school-wide plan to address prosocial behaviors, respect for one another, pinpoint settings where problems occur and revise supervision of these areas as needed.

Necessary Prerequisites

An experienced city fire chief, in response to a question on how his department spends its time said, "We spend about 80% of our time in educational efforts to prevent fires and about 20% of our time in fighting fires." In a similar vein, a school or district should spend most of its time in developing steps designed to prevent emergency situations and the remainder of its efforts in responding to crises in a timely, safe and efficient manner. The following steps are presented as necessary prerequisites for establishing safe schools, and for ensuring adequate school emergency procedures.

Safe Physical Environment. The physical layout of a school property, building and grounds, can make a school vulnerable or resistant to school safety issues (Crowe, 1990). School properties need to be assessed for safety concerns such as ease of surveillance, obstructions to adequate supervision in certain areas, (for example, playgrounds, parking lots, and restrooms), security systems and communication systems.

Community Coordination. Many risk factors for school safety are often found in the school neighborhood such as poverty, crime rates, drug trafficking and other criminal activity. It makes good sense to coordinate the school's efforts with the various community agencies involved with providing services for these risk factors (Hawkins & Catalano, 1992). These agencies include police, social service agencies, juvenile justice system, church groups and volunteer organizations. It is highly desirable for school personnel to develop good communications with these community groups and to coordinate services where appropriate.

Proactive School-Wide Discipline Plans. A growing body of research has shown that systematic implementation of positive and proactive school-wide discipline plans not only improve the school learning environment, but also significantly impact on school safety (Colvin, Kame'enui, & Sugai, 1993; Horner, Sugai, & Horner, 2000). These plans involve systematically teaching appropriate behavior and provide necessary support for all students.

Strong focus on academic achievement. Schools and school districts that provide a major focus on improving school academic achievement have discovered that school success becomes a deterrent to school alienation and subsequent violence (Walker, Colvin, & Ramsey, 1995).

Staff and Student Training. Staff needs to be given systematic professional development in the areas of crisis prevention. Several video programs and training materials are available for these purposes (Colvin, 1999; Colvin, 2001; Dwyer, Osher, & Warger, 1998; Embry & Flannery, 1994; Stephens, 1995).

Moreover, schools are well used to fire drills and, in some areas, earthquake drills. In the same way, staff and students need sufficient practice for emergency procedures. Each staff person and student should know exactly what is required of them during an emergency and these roles need to be practiced regularly to maximize order and safety during an emergency.

Development of a Crisis or Emergency Response Plan. A school crisis plan needs to be carefully developed, written up and disseminated to staff, students, parents, community members, and agencies as appropriate (Paine & Sprague, 2000). The plans need to include specific details of communication procedures, roles and responsibilities of all stake-holders, and formation of a crisis response team.

Action Response Plan

All of the preceding information in this chapter has been focused on factors in a school that are designed to prevent emergency situations and to create a readiness to respond should an emergency arise. The current section focuses on the steps school personnel take in order to actually respond to a crisis, that is, the components of a *crisis action response plan.* Actions taken by the response team are usually divided into two parts: *(a)* Those responses that must occur *immediately,* as soon as the emergency situation arises; and *(b)* Those responses that must be taken *within the first hour* (Paine & Sprague, 2000). A sample checklist for an action response plan is presented in Appendix J: Form 8.1.

Appendix J

Form 8.1: Sample Checklist for School Emergency Action Response Plan

1. Immediate

____ Assess life and safety issues immediately.

____ Provide immediate emergency care as needed.

____ Call 911 and notify police (and rescue people as needed).

____ Secure all areas.

____ Alert school staff of the situation with directions for their roles.

____ Implement protection procedures as necessary such as lock-down or evacuation.

____ Implement dismissal procedures as planned, if needed.

____ Contact school district office, especially the superintendent.

2. Within the First Hour

____ Convene the crisis team to ensure immediate steps have been taken and then identify all the necessary subsequent steps to be followed, designating the person in charge of each step.

____ Identify necessary and available resources that need to be utilized.

____ Implement communication procedures.

____ Alert persons in charge of communications, especially to avoid confusion and misinformation.

____ Notify parents and appropriate community agencies.

____ Contact district public relations office and prepare a measured statement for public dissemination.

Adapted from: Paine & Sprague, 2000, 10-11.

Follow-Up

Once the initial response to an emergency situation has occurred, several critical follow-up steps need to be implemented. At one level, there is a strong desire for staff and students to return to the normal routines of a school day. However, it is also very important that support structures are in place for affected students and staff and that a thorough review of the response plan is conducted to assess the effectiveness of the plan and to make revisions as necessary.

Support Plans. The support plans for affected students will vary according to the nature and extent of the particular emergency. It may be necessary to establish a safe room where *students* may receive individual counseling services. Part of the school emergency plan requires that a pool of support personnel be identified and procedures set up for them to be immediately available for crisis situations.

Support services need to be available for several weeks as some students may need long term care and other students may experience delayed reactions and need assistance some time after the critical event. It is also very important to monitor students as there may be differential responses to the emergency situation. Some students may be deeply affected and may need more in depth assistance and support than is available in the school setting.

Support services should also be made available to staff, especially staff members involved in the emergency situation and staff members who may have a particular professional relationship with students involved in the crisis such as the homeroom teacher, classroom teacher, or coach. Moreover, care and attention must be provided to the service support personnel as their task can be particularly taxing.

Communication with Staff. Because crisis situations are relatively rare, thank goodness, it is very important for the school administration to carefully and fully apprise staff of the necessary details concerning the crisis and specific procedures that are to be implemented. In this way rumors, possible exaggerations, or understatements may be promulgated. It is in everyone's best interest to have consistent and accurate information.

Emergency Response Plan Evaluation. Usually after two weeks following an emergency, an evaluation of the response plan needs to occur. The first question to be asked is, "Did everyone follow the procedures as written and as rehearsed?" Any breakdowns need to be noted and appropriate follow-up should occur. Secondly, it is important to identify the strengths and weaknesses of the plan. That is, which parts of the plan were effective and efficient and which parts were inadequate. Finally, revisions to the plan need to occur, as needed, and adjustments need to be documented in the written plan and rehearsals conducted to ensure that the school community is familiar with the changes. It is highly desirable to develop checklists for these evaluations. Several examples of checklists are presented in the following resource list. A sample checklist and action plan are presented in Appendix K: Form 8.2 and Appendix L: Form 8.3.

Appendix K

Form 8.2: School Crisis/Emergency Response Checklist[1]

Date of Assessment:

Person(s) Completing Assessment:

Check status of each item (in place, partially in place, not in place).

In-Place Status			
Fully	Partially	Not	Item
			1. Crisis response team identified
			2. Home-school-community linkage
			3. Proactive school-wide discipline system
			4. High rates of academic & social success
			5. Clear written policy & procedures
			6. Regular, supervised opportunities to practice (staff and students)
			7. Posted generic response sequence
			8. Designated safe areas
			9. Clear roles & responsibilities of key personnel
			10. Clear fool-proof communication system
			11. Means of securing immediate external support
			12. Procedures for securing or locking down classroom or school
			13. Posted instructions for unique situations
			14. Procedures for accounting for whereabouts of all students & staff
			15. Systematic process for conducting investigations
			16. Clear policy on physical interventions
			17. Procedures for documenting dangerous & potentially dangerous situations

[1]Complete checklist at least quarterly.

Source: Sugai & Colvin, 1999.

Appendix L

Form 8.3: School Crisis/Emergency Response Action Plan

Team Present in Developing Action Plan:			
1. Overall status	High	Medium	Low
2. List three major strengths	a.		
	b.		
	c.		
3. List three major areas in need of improvement	a.		
	b.		
4. Circle the area <u>most</u> in need of improvement	c.		
5. Develop an <u>Action Plan</u> for circled area	Step 1:	Who:_____ When:_____	
	Step 2:	Who:_____ When:_____	
	Step 3:	Who:_____ When:_____	
	Step 4:	Who:_____ When:_____	
	Step 5:	Who:_____ When:_____	
	Step 6:	Who:_____ When:_____	
6. Schedule next self-assessment	Who:_____	When: _____	

Source: Sugai & Colvin, 1999.

Systematic Monitoring of Incidents. It is very important for a school to keep accurate data on incidents involving emergency situations. In this way staff may be able to identify patterns for recurring incidents. These patterns may set the occasion for specific analyses such as a school-wide assessment and intervention, functional analyses for individual students, long term planning for individual students and possibly referral to other forms of evaluation, such as for special education or services involving community agencies.

Box 8.2: Resource Material for Preventing and Managing School Emergencies

Videos

Colvin, G. (2001). *Managing threats: A school-wide action plan* (Video program). Eugene, OR: Iris Media.

Colvin, G. (1999). *Defusing anger and aggression: Safe strategies for secondary school educators* (Video program). Eugene, OR: Iris Media.

Books and Manuals

Crowe, T. D. (1990). Designing safe schools. *School Safety,* Fall.

Dwyer, K., Osher, D., & Warger, C. (1998). *Early warning, timely response: A guide to safe schools.* Washington, D.C.: U.S. Department of Education.

Embry, D. D., & Flannery, D. J. (1994). *Peacebuilders— Reducing youth violence: A working application of cognitive-social-imitative competence research.* Tucson, AZ: Heartsprings, Inc.

Paine, C., & Sprague, J. (2000). Crisis prevention and response: Is your school prepared? *Oregon School Study Council, 43*(2). Eugene, OR: Institute on Violence and Destructive Behavior, University of Oregon.

Stephens, R.D. (1995). *Safe Schools: A handbook for violence prevention.* Bloomington, IN: National Education Service.

Watson, R., Poda, J., Miller, C., Rice, E., & West, G. (1990). *Containing crises: A guide to managing school emergencies.* Bloomington, IN: National Education Service.

Articles

Horner, R. H., Sugai, G., & Horner, H. F. (2000). A schoolwide approach to student discipline, *The School Administrator, 57*(2), 20-23.

Sugai, G., & Colvin, G. (1999). *Primer on crises and emergency responses.* Eugene, OR: PBIS, College of Education, University of Oregon.

Chapter Summary

Developing emergency procedures is probably one of the least satisfying responsibilities facing educators today. Obviously no one wants a school crisis. However, it is universally accepted that no one is exempt from school crises. Consequently, school districts and all schools are obligated to develop written emergency procedures, attend to the various prerequisite steps, develop a crisis team, prepare an action response plan and attend to the various follow-up activities. In this way school personnel take a very important and necessary step towards helping to provide their staff and students with a supportive environment necessary for learning and school safety. Additional resources for preventing and managing emergency behavior are listed in Box 8.2.

CHAPTER 9

REINTERGRATION STRATEGIES FOR MANAGING DE-ESCALATION PHASE

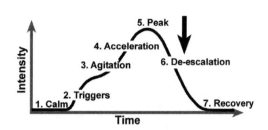

The sixth phase in the model for acting-out behavior provides a series of steps to bring students down from the serious acting-out behavior of Peak Phase to resumption of normal activities. This transition phase is called De-escalation.

When a student is engaged in serious acting-out behavior of the Peak Phase, such as sustained disruption, violence, and severe tantrums, the period may seem interminable for the staff persons involved. However, the student's behavior will eventually subside either as a result of the strategies used to manage the peak behavior or simply as a function of exhaustion (Yasutake, 1995). Typically, the student is in a subdued or somewhat confused state following a serious behavioral episode. One explanation is that when students are engaged in out-of-control behavior they are not thinking clearly. In other words, their behavior is driven or conditioned. The emotions of anger or frustration take control for a short period of time (Bower, 1992; Isen, 1984). The classic example is rage. When persons experience rage, they are not making decisions or thinking how they will respond. Rather their behavior is excessively compulsive and when the episode is over there is a change of state or quieting down. This period, De-escalation, is sometimes called *reintegration*. The reason is that the individual is in the process of resuming normal emotional and intellectual functioning following an episode of being out-of-control.

The following steps are designed, in sequence, to manage the student's behavior immediately following the serious incidents of the Peak Phase: *(a)* Isolate the student; *(b)* Engage in independent work with clear criteria; *(c)* Complete exit paperwork as appropriate; *(d)* Restore the environment as applicable; and *(e)* Resume the regular schedule.

Step One: Isolate the Student

The first intervention following a serious incident is to *isolate* the student with adequate *supervision*. Here are some guidelines for implementing this step:

Choose a Location. It is strongly recommended that a designated location be chosen ahead of time for this purpose. For example, a small room, corner of a room, corner of a room with a divider, or section of another room could be used. It is very important the location for the isolated time is away from the flow of traffic and other stimulation.

Provide Adequate Supervision. Keep in mind that adequate supervision needs to be provided at all times, as the student may regress to exhibiting serious acting-out behavior.

Cool-Down Time. The primary purpose for isolation is to provide the student with an opportunity to cool down or become more collected. Within a few moments, separated from other students and class activities, the involved student will have more opportunity to reflect on his or her serious behavior. Moreover, it is important to separate the student from other students to prevent inappropriate interactions or face-saving behavior.

Length of Time. The amount of time that a student needs to cool down will vary from student to student and will also depend of the gravity of the acting-out behavior. A student who exhibited severe acting-out behavior will need more time than a student who exhibited less serious behavior. Typically a student should be left alone in the range of five to ten minutes. It is not desirable to leave the student alone for long periods. Many students with serious emotional disturbances do not have the cognitive skills or emotional control to process the critical events and may begin to panic or become very restless and confused when left alone for long periods following a serious incident. The supervisor should make himself or herself seen by the student on a periodic basis during this isolation time. There is no need for interactions, however, the mere presence of the supervisor will help to provide security or assurance for the more emotionally involved student.

Step Two: Decision to Send the Student Home or Retain the Student

Depending on arrangements, school resources, district resources and severity of the behavior problems exhibited in the Peak Phase, the student may be sent home. In these cases it is recommended that the student complete Step One above and then leave the school or setting. Clearly a student should not be sent home in a highly agitated state or when still engaged in the serious acting-out behavior. If the decision has been made to send the student home, then once the student has settled down and the parent or designee has

Reintegration:
Student piecing things together.

Source: IRIS Media, Inc.

arrived, then the student may be released. The debriefing session described at the end of Chapter 7 should be conducted as soon as possible after the student returns to school.

If the decision has been made to retain the student in the school setting and to return the student to class or current school activity, then continue with the following steps.

Step Three: Engage in Independent Work with Clear Criteria

Once the student has regained some sense of composure, the next step is to provide the student with some tasks, specifically some independent work. The primary reason for introducing independent work at this stage is to help the student *regain focus.* In the earlier section of this book, the primary behavioral characteristic displayed by students in this phase was described as *confusion.* One reason for this disposition is that the acting-out incident is often an emotional outburst with little thinking involved (Bower, 1992; Isen, 1984, Yasutake, 1995). Consequently, as the student recovers, thinking processes begin to function slowly. Independent work activities provide the student with a relatively "safe focus." In this way the student has something to attend to which helps self-management of the transition from being out-of-control to recovery.

The following guidelines are designed to ensure that the independent work assigned to the involved student assists the student to recover:

Probe Level of Cooperation. If the student undertakes the independent work, the teacher is given reliable information that he or she is recovering and getting back on track. There is a very good chance that the student will cooperate with the remaining steps. If, however, the student refuses to engage in the independent work, the teacher is given information that the student needs more time to calm down and settle. In this case the student should be given more time to either cool down or to complete the tasks.

Ensure the Student has Mastery of the Task. It is critical that the student can complete the independent work with at least 90% accuracy. This is not an occasion to challenge the student with new or near new learning. Rather, it is work that is designed to help the student to regain focus. Consequently, work should be selected that is simply review and practice.

Choose Tasks that Require Active Responses. Again, tasks are selected to ensure that the student is physically active and engaging such as writing down definitions from a dictionary for an older student, or coloring a page for a younger student. By contrast, passive tasks such as reading a chapter of a book may set the stage for the student to disengage or daydream, making it more difficult for the student to become focused and productive.

Set a Reasonable Standard for Completion. It is also very important for the teacher to make reasonable demands on the quality or accuracy of the work completed by the student. For example, the teacher might expect a page of writing with reasonable penmanship in the 15 minutes allocated. If the student completes the page and the penmanship is acceptable, the teacher can conclude that the student is cooperating and may move to the next step. However if the student, for example, has completed only a quarter of a page and the writing is way below her normal standard, the teacher may conclude that the student it not ready to move to the next step. It is crucial to stay with this task until it is completed to a satisfactory standard. Otherwise, if the teacher moves to the next step, the student will continue to display non-cooperation and the situation may escalate or at least remain at this level of non-cooperation impeding the steps to recovery.

Step Four: Complete Exit Paperwork as Appropriate to Adequate Criterion

Paperwork is necessary to document the student's behavior and to provide information for the debriefing session (Recovery Phase, next chapter). Such information is usually collected in the form of an incident report or office referral describing the behavior and its relevant circumstances. It is also very helpful to have the student complete some form of standardized *behavior form* to be used in the debriefing process. Two commonly used behavior forms are presented, Appendix M: Form 9.1 and Appendix N: Form 9.2.

Appendix M

Form 9.1: Behavior Form for Debriefing Process

Student Name: _____ Date: _____

1. What was your behavior?

   _____

   _____

   _____

2. What was your concern or need?

   _____

   _____

   _____

3. What could you do next time that would be acceptable?

   _____

   _____

   _____

4. What are you expected to do next?

   _____

   _____

   _____

5. Can you do it appropriately?   ___ Yes ___ No

   Student signature   _____

   Teacher signature   _____

Source: Walker, Colvin, & Ramsey, 1995.

Appendix N

Form 9.2: Incident Debriefing Behavior Form

Student Name: Date:

1. What was your behavior?

   _____

   _____

2. What did you want?
   - ___ I wanted attention from others
   - ___ I wanted to be in control of the situation
   - ___ I wanted to challenge the teacher
   - ___ I wanted to avoid doing my work
   - ___ I wanted to be sent home
   - ___ I wanted to cause problems because I am having a bad day
   - ___ I wanted to get back at others because they don't like me
   - ___ I wanted revenge
   - ___ I wanted_____

3. Did you get what you wanted? ___ Yes ___ No

   Explain _____

   _____

   _____

4. What are you required to do next?_____

   _____

   _____

5. Will you be able to do it appropriately? ___ Yes ___ No

   Why? _____

   _____

   Signature:

Time started:	Time ended:
Given by:	Number of minutes:
Reviewed by:	Time added:
Class:	**Total time owed:**

                                        Geoff Colvin

In addition to providing information to use in the debriefing session conducted in the next phase, Recovery, the actual *process* of completing the behavior form serves as an important intervention. A common concern reported by educators who deal with students who exhibit acting-out behavior is the issue of student ownership or student accountability. In many cases, students will either deny their behavior or blame others, thereby justifying their behavior. The first item on the debriefing behavior forms ask the question, "What was your behavior?" To answer this question, the student has to admit what he or she has done and name the behavior exhibited in the Peak Phase. Once the student admits the behavior, the debriefing process and recovery steps fall into place more readily. However, if the student resists completing the form, then the next steps in the process are not likely to be completed successfully.

It is important to realize that just because students cooperate with the cool-down step and complete the independent work tasks, we cannot assume they will automatically complete the behavior form. The reason is that students may be bothered still by some aspect of the previous incident and may react to having to admit their behavior. It is crucial that the supervisor remain persistent, but not in a hurry for the student to complete the form adequately. In many cases, students may need some assistance or shaping to actually name their behavior as required in item1. The supervisor needs to make certain that the student completes the first item to a reasonable degree of accuracy. It is often necessary, in the case of an unsatisfactory response, to direct the student to re-do the form and provide the student with brief and simple feedback. In Box 9.1 an example of successive responses from a student are presented with the corresponding feedback from the teacher resulting in acceptable completion of item 1 from Form 9.1 or 9.2.

1. What was your behavior?

_____

_____

Box 9.1: Example of Successive Student Responses to Item 1 on Behavior Form 9.1 and Corresponding Shaping Feedback from the Teacher

Attempt 1

Behavior Form for Debriefing Process (Form 9.1)

1. **What was your behavior?**
Student: *"Randy hit me with the f... pool stick and I stopped the a...."*

Teacher feedback: *"Tim you have made a response. Thank you. But listen. The language is not OK. We will have to do it over without the bad language."*

Attempt 2

1. **What was your behavior?**
Student: *"My behavior was OK under the circumstances."*

Teacher feedback: *"Tim, thank you for using acceptable language."* (Pause). *"But listen, you haven't said what you did. I understand you hit or did something physical with Randy. So we need to see something like that."* (Gets another form.)

Attempt 3

1. **What was your behavior?**
Student: *"Randy was gonna hit me with the pool stick so I grabbed him fast and made out I was trying to hit him. I wanted to."*

Teacher feedback: *"Thank you Tim. You said what you did and we will talk about this more fully later on."* (Teacher proceeds to next step.)

Step Five: Determine Consequences

Given the student has exhibited serious behavior, consequences need to be delivered. The reason is that the consequences are designed to provide feedback to the student that his or her behavior is unacceptable and should not occur again. The consequences should be tied to the context if possible. For example, if the behavior occurred during recess then the student may miss recess a number of times or have a restricted recess. In Tim's case, Box 9.1, the behavior occurred in the recreation room so he could be banned from the recreation room for a number of days.

Step Six: Restore the Environment if Appropriate

It is very helpful in terms of student accountability for the student to restore the environment where appropriate. For example, if the student trashed a room, he or she may be required to help rearrange the room and pick up any mess. Or, if the student kicked over the garbage can and threw

Geoff Colvin

a bat into the wall, he or she may be required to pick up the can, retrieve the bat and put it in its proper place. Obviously, if it is necessary to have the environment restored for immediate use by other students, this step cannot be used.

In some cases, there is value in having the student do some community service activity either at this time or later. For example, if the student made a mess in the library and the library needed to be restored immediately, this student may be required to help in the library with some small task such as straightening chairs. In this way, the student receives feedback that if you do something that inconveniences others then you should make some contribution to rectify the situation.

Step Seven: Resume Regular Schedule

At this point the student has been given an opportunity to settle down and has cooperated with a series of tasks (independent work completing a product to a reasonable standard, filling out the behavior form with reliable information, and restoring the environment as appropriate). As a result, the student is likely to cooperate when returned to class. This process of systematically building cooperation has been referred to as a concept of behavioral momentum (Mace, Hock, Lalli, West, Belfiore, Pinter, & Brown, 1988; Mace, 1996; Sanchez-Fort, Brady, & Davis, 1995; Singer, Singer, & Horner, 1987). In effect, the student has completed this phase of the acting-out cycle, De-escalation, and is now ready to enter the final phase, *Recovery.*

Chapter Summary

The De-escalation Phase is a transition from serious acting-out behavior, *Peak Phase* to *Recovery Phase.* The De-escalation period does not last very long, which means that the timing in applying strategies is crucial for successful implementation. The primary purpose of these strategies is to help the student to regain composure and to provide a focus on cooperation. It is recommended to present the strategies in the prescribed order. The reason is that each step is designed to obtain increasing levels of cooperation so that when the student exits this phase, there is a reasonable chance that the student will cooperate when he or she resumes normal activities in the next phase, Recovery.

CHAPTER 10

RESUMPTION STRATEGIES FOR RECOVERY PHASE

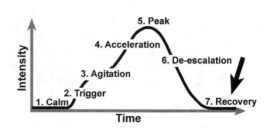

In this final phase, *Recovery*, the students are back in the normal schedule. It is very important to understand that just because the student had regained composure and was cooperating in the previous phase, De-escalation, there is no guarantee that the student will maintain cooperation in the normal schedule. The reason is that the student regained composure and focus in *another setting.* That is the student is coming from an isolated setting to the normal regular classroom setting. There is some chance that the students may respond to the returning student in a way that is inflammatory (either deliberately or unwittingly). Or, the stimuli that set off the original acting-out cycle may still be present, such as certain students, staff or tasks. Consequently, there are some additional steps and strategies to assist the student in overcoming these potential problems and resume the normal class routines with success.

There are two main parts for the strategies in this Recovery Phase: *(a)* Transition steps; and *(b)* Debriefing plan.

Transition Steps

The transition steps are designed to build on the strategies used in the previous phase, De-escalation, to ensure the student's composure, focus and cooperation is strengthened. The following steps are recommended:

Provide Strong Focus on Normal Routines. The main intent here is to engage the student in the present class activity as soon as possible. The immediate goal is to assist the student to re-enter the classroom activity and maintain a high rate of on-task behavior. Prompts, verbal reinforcement, contacts and offers to assist as needed should be provided.

Sometimes the student may want to talk about the incident, such as what may have happened, who is at fault and what happened to the other participants in the problem. In these cases it is best to assure the student that these issues, and others, will be fully addressed later on in the debriefing session.

It may also happen that the student will appear to be uncomfortable in class, look a little sheepish or embarrassed and may have difficulty participating in class. This situation could be confounded if the class is engaged in a group activity involving discussion. In this case, the teacher may offer the student an option of doing some individual or independent catch-up work.

Do Not Negotiate about the Consequences for the Serious Behavior. Some students who exhibit severe behavior may have learned that if they cooperate fully in class following a serious incident, they can negotiate about the consequences for their serious behavior. For example, a student may be required to miss recess for several days because he or she became involved in a serious incident resulting in the student punching another student. The offending student, on returning to class cooperated fully and after the third day says, " I have been very good in class, can I go to recess now?" It is very important for the teacher to maintain the consequences. Otherwise, the students learn that no matter what behavior they exhibit, they can negotiate on the consequences as long as they cooperate when they return to class. The consequences are designed to teach limits, that is, to provide feedback to the students that the behavior is unacceptable. However, teachers should acknowledge cooperation by using other reinforcers, not by modifying consequences for previous serious behavior. For example, in response to the student above, the teacher might say, "Michael, I am very pleased that you are doing great work. But listen, you are missing recess for five days because you punched someone. So please keep up the good work and let's not have any punching at recess when your five days are up. OK."

Strongly Acknowledge Occurrences of Problem Solving Behaviors. When students make chronic errors in academic subjects, teachers are ready to strongly praise them for correct responses. The same practice should apply to problem behavior. When a student displays appropriate responses to certain situations that typically trigger problem behavior for the student, the teacher should be ready to provide strong reinforcement. For example, Sarah has had a number of serious incidents arising from being asked to re-do certain areas of report writing following corrections. On this occasion, Sarah received her report that contained a number of errors and sections to be re-written. Sarah calmly re-wrote the required sections and made the corrections that were suggested. The teacher approached her and thanked her very strongly for attending to the corrections, "Sarah, thank you so much for getting these corrections completed. I know this is hard for you. Great job!"

Communicate Support and Expectation that the Students Can Succeed. Students who exhibit acting-out behavior on a regular basis usually have little confidence that they can be successful in their attempts to change behavior. Many of them have already been exposed to several behavior plans, counseling and exhortations and their problem behavior persists. Once the student is in the Recovery Phase it is very important for the teacher to: *(a)* Encourage the student to keep trying; *(b)* Identify how the teacher can be supportive and help the student succeed; and *(c)* Specify how they can work together as a team so that the student can be successful.

Establish a Specific Plan if Necessary. The debriefing session usually results in an agreement that the student will undertake certain problem-solving activities (essentially to identify the triggers and select an alternative response for each). The teacher should ensure that the plan is sufficiently concrete and that a monitoring and review schedule is established.

Recovery Phase: Teacher provides encouragement.

Photo by: Kylee Colvin

Geoff Colvin

Debriefing Plan

It is quite standard for teachers to deliver negative consequences when students exhibit inappropriate behavior. In most cases, these consequences are sufficient to change the student's behavior. However, in some cases, such as those involving students who exhibit chronic acting-out behavior, the student returns to the original setting and it is not long before the student exhibits the same problem behavior. In this event the teacher may deliver stronger or different negative consequences, only to find that the problem behavior persists, or worse, intensifies. In effect an unproductive *cycle* of problem behavior and negative consequences develops. One powerful way to prevent this cycle is to include a *debriefing* activity that follows the prescribed negative consequences (Sugai & Colvin, 1997). This step is designed to help the student understand the dynamics of the problem behavior cycle and to prepare the student to exhibit appropriate behavior in the future especially in the presence of the triggering events.

Debriefing has often been called a feedback session, problem solving meeting or exit interview and is similar in many respects to Life Space Interviewing procedures described by Wood (1990). Debriefing strategies represent critical opportunities for students to review the context of important events that may have contributed to the serious acting-out behavior and equip the student to manage these events appropriately in the future.

The debriefing strategy *should not* be used as an aversive consequence, that is, a carry-over from the negative consequences that may have been delivered to the student for his or her behavior. Rather, debriefing is fundamentally a *proactive* strategy designed to help the student problem solve. The debriefing strategy has three essential features: *(a)* Review the problem incident so as to highlight the triggering events; *(b)* Establish alternative acceptable responses to these triggering events to replace the problem behavior; and *(c)* Provide a focus on a smooth transition from the interview to the current classroom activity.

Generally, it is desirable to conduct the debriefing session after the student has been on track in the classroom for at least 20 minutes and preferably the same day as the occurrence of the incident. Typically, if the classroom teacher conducts the debriefing, the session should take somewhere in the range of three to five minutes. To facilitate consistent and efficient application of the debriefing strategy and to obtain a record of the discussion, it is very useful to use a written checklist or form. Moreover, when the student participates in the completion of the form, greater student ownership is established. A sample form is presented in Appendix 0: Form 10.1. Guidelines for completing the form with the student are presented in Box 10.2 followed by an example of a completed checklist and plan, Box 10.3.

Box 10.1: Guidelines for Conducting the Debriefing Session Using Debriefing Form 10.1

A. Complete the top portion of Debriefing Form 10.1.

B. Explain the purpose of the debriefing session emphasizing the focus on problem solving.

C. Ensure the student understands each question, 1–5.

D. Have the student complete questions 1–5; provide assistance as needed.

E. Ensure the writing is reasonably legible.

F. Have the student read responses 1–5 when the form is completed.

G. Provide practice opportunities as needed to ensure the student knows exactly what is required in the future.

H. Ask student to sign the form and sign it yourself.

I. Schedule additional reviews as needed, possibly weekly.

J. End session with focus on being successful and encourage student to try his or best.

K. Direct student to next class activity.

L. Make copies and distribute as appropriate to involved staff and parent(s).

M. Within 48 hours review the debriefing form with student and discuss progress.

N. End all subsequent sessions offering encouragement and support to student.

Appendix O

Form 10.1: Debriefing Form

Student Name: Grade: Room:

Classroom Teacher: Date:

Staff Member conducting debriefing session
(if different from Classroom Teacher):

1. What did **you** do? _____

    _____

    _____

    _____

2. What, when, and why did the problem occur? _____

    _____

    _____

    _____

3. What will <u>you </u>do next time instead of the problem behavior? _____

    _____

    _____

    _____

4. What do you need to do next after we complete this form? _____

    _____

    _____

    _____

5. Do you need help to take the next step? _____

    _____

    _____

    _____

Student Signature_____   Staff Signature_____

Appendix O

Form 10.1: Debriefing Form

Student Name: *Caesar Romano* Grade: *7* Room: *210*

Classroom Teacher: *Mrs. Henry* Date: *January 10, 2004*

Staff Member conducting debriefing session
(if different from Classroom Teacher):

1. What did **you** do? _____

I threw my math book at the wall and cussed out the teacher.

_____

_____

2. What, when, and why did the problem occur? *I couldn't do the math. It*
was too hard. I asked Erica for help and was told to stop talking and get
on with it myself. I didn't want to stay after to do it. How can I do it if
it is too hard? It's not fair!

3. What will <u>you</u> do next time instead of the problem behavior? _____

I have to get help the right way. Put up my hand.

_____

_____

4. What do you need to do next after we complete this form? _____

Continue with the rest of the math problems.

_____

_____

5. Do you need help to take the next step? *No. I can do it myself.*

_____

_____

_____

Student Signature *Caesar Romano*   Staff Signature *Mrs. Henry*

Chapter Summary

The overall objective for the strategies in the Recovery Phase is to continue the transition from the De-escalation Phase to full participation in the current classroom activities and to effectively problem solve through a simple debriefing process with the student on how to respond appropriately to future events. The debriefing process is designed for students who display chronic problem behavior, especially those students who exhibit the cycle of acting-out behavior. In these cases, negative consequences by themselves are insufficient in helping the students to exhibit appropriate behavior in similar future circumstances. The debriefing strategy is designed to help the student to pinpoint the critical events that may have contributed to the acting-out incident and then to teach or establish acceptable replacement behaviors for similar situations in the future.

Section Three—

Conclusion

The information in this book is for teachers and service providers who must cope with and provide an education for students who display serious acting-out behavior. The material is designed to enhance educators' understanding of problem behavior, particularly as it relates to student-teacher interactions. This book also provides descriptions of many best-practice procedures and research-based practices that can be readily implemented safely in classrooms and school settings. The author hopes that the content of this book will serve as a practical tool for assisting teachers in their most valuable work with these high needs students.

CHAPTER 11

SUMMARY AND CASE STUDY

Summary

Acting-out behavior can be described by a seven-phase conceptual model. Specific behaviors can be identified for each phase of this model. Behavioral descriptions were culled from a large sample of students who exhibit this behavioral pattern. The primary purpose of classifying behavior in this way is to enable practitioners to understand the behavioral processes involved in escalating interactions between teachers and students. The descriptions tell the teachers which problematic student behavior to expect at each stage of potentially explosive situations that have, unfortunately, become a fact of daily school life.

Strategies and procedures are described for managing student behavior at each phase in the cycle. The basic intent of the strategies is to arrest the behavior at that point in the chain, thereby preventing further escalation and, at the same time, set the stage for students to engage in appropriate alternative behavior. The overall emphasis is on identifying the early behaviors in the chain, redirecting the students toward appropriate behavior, and subsequently preempting the acting-out cycle of serious behavior. In Phases One through Four (Calm, Triggers, Agitation and Acceleration), the emphasis is on effective teaching and proactive management practices. In the remaining phases, the emphasis is in safety, crisis management and follow-up.

A form presented in Chapter 2, Appendix B: Form 2.2, can be used for developing a comprehensive behavior support plan for students who exhibit serious acting-out behavior. This form has three general applications: *(a)* At a staff meeting where teachers develop a plan of action for an individual student; *(b)* In a parent-teacher meeting where the parent, with the help of the teacher or consultant, develops a plan for implementation in the student's home; and *(c)* As a self-management tool for students, with assistance from the teacher as needed, to identify their behaviors at each phase in the cycle and to identify corresponding strategies for changing their behavior.

Form 2.2: Behavior Support Plan

Student Name: *Kyle Jacobsen*   Date: *11/16/03*

Home Room Teacher: *Walt Jones*   Grade: *5th*

Staff Present: *Andrea Cole, Fred Carpenter, Wilson McCoy, Maieta Stephensen, Walt Jones*

ASSESSMENT	STRATEGIES
Calm *Likes to help* *Displays successful work* *Enjoys games* *Loves the computer*	Calm
Triggers *Repeating tasks* *Teasing remarks and put-downs from other students* *Facing corrections* *When he is given consequences for misbehavior*	Triggers
Agitation *Walks around the room* *Scowls at other students* *Pouts and mumbles to himself* *Does not concentrate on his work* *Complains about other students bothering him*	Agitation
Acceleration *Argues and will not quit* *Defiant and noncompliant "Make me"* *Name calls and threatens students* *Raises voice and shouts*	Acceleration
Peak *Throws objects around the room* *Kicks furniture* *Hits others students* *Threatens teacher* *Leaves room yelling and screaming*	Peak
De-escalation *Goes very quiet and puts head down* *If he leaves the room he hides and* *curls up in a corner somewhere* *Talks to himself negatively, "No one likes me," "I'm a loser."* *Likes to fiddle with things*	De-escalation
Recovery *Quite subdued* *Likes to work alone* *Looks depressed but tries to do some work* *Likes to draw*	Recovery

Case Study

We return now to the behavior support plan for an individual student introduced in Chapter 2, Box 2.9. At this point the assessment part of the behavior support plan was completed. The other component, strategies corresponding to each phase in the acting-out cycle, will now be added to complete the plan. A recapitulation of the student's behavioral history will be provided followed by a completed behavior support plan for this student.

Background. Kyle is a 10-year-old fifth grade student who has had a long history of problem behavior in public schools. Numerous incidents of acting-out behavior include: threatening and abusing staff; throwing chairs and materials around the room; hitting other students at recess; engaging in serious disruptive tantrums; and leaving the school building when he is very angry. Teachers say he has a very short fuse and is easily upset. His grades show he is below average in all subjects yet he is of average to above-average intelligence. He lives with his mother. For some periods of his life he lived with his grandmother and in foster care. After attending several different schools, he was evaluated for special education and placed in a self-contained classroom for students with behavior problems. His mother has steadfastly refused to consent to placement outside his area school. She maintains he is basically a good child but has his bad moments. He was on Ritalin when he lived with his grandmother, but now his mother has terminated medication because it makes him worse, she says. Presently, he is placed in a resource room for reading and math and is in general education classrooms for all other subjects.

A staff meeting was called. The strategies component of his behavior support plan was completed by the group (Box 11.1). Over a period of one term of implementation, Kyle's incidents of serious problem behavior dropped from three per week to one for the last two weeks of term. His attendance at school increased from an average of 3.2 to 4.9 days per week. He is now full time in general education classrooms and receives monitoring (periodic checks) in math and reading.

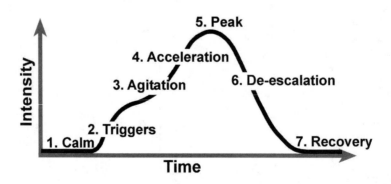

Box 11.1 Complete Behavior Support Plan
Appendix B

Form 2.2: Behavior Support Plan

Student Name: *Kyle Jacobsen*   Date: *11/16/03*

Home Room Teacher: *Walt Jones*   Grade: *5th*

Staff Present: *Andrea Cole, Fred Carpenter, Wilson McCoy, Maieta Stephensen, Walt Jones*

ASSESSMENT	STRATEGIES
Calm *Likes to help* *Displays successful work* *Enjoys games* *Loves the computer*	**Calm** *Contract for successful work* *Include computer time in contract* *Assist with distributing materials*
Triggers *Repeating tasks* *Teasing remarks and put-downs from other students* *Facing corrections* *When he is given consequences for misbehavior*	**Triggers** *Precorrection plan for corrections* *Coaching on ignoring and not respondng to teasing*
Agitation *Walks around the room* *Scowls at other students* *Pouts and mumbles to himself* *Does not concentrate on his work* *Complains about other students bothering him*	**Agitation** *Option of quiet area* *Use jobs or errands* *Increase teacher contact*
Acceleration *Argues and will not quit* *Defiant and noncompliant "Make me"* *Name calls and threatens students* *Raises voice and shouts*	**Acceleration** *Teacher to avoid discussion when he argues—Teacher to delay responding to name calling and mild disruptive behavior—Provide reminders and prompts for how to get attention and assistance—Use 3-step limit-testing strategy when he persists with mild disruptive behavior after 5-10 minutes*
Peak *Throws objects around the room* *Kicks furniture* *Hits others students* *Threatens teacher* *Leaves room yelling and screaming*	**Peak** *Prompt other students to stay on task at onset of his disruptive behavior—Use room clear procedures—Use code 1 emergency procedures for unsafe behavior*
De-escalation *Goes very quiet and puts head down* *If he leaves the room he hides and curls up in a corner somewhere* *Talks to himself negatively, "No one likes me," "I'm a loser"* *Likes to fiddle with things*	**De-escalation** *Leave alone in isolation with supervision* *Present a math sheet after 10 minutes of cool down* *Present behavior form for debriefing process* *Restore room where possible then exit classroom* *Begin classroom activity with independent work*
Recovery *Quite subdued* *Likes to work alone* *Looks depressed but tries to do some work* *Likes to draw*	**Recovery** *Provide independent work for short time* *Conduct debriefing session* *Reinforce on-task behavior—Provide encouragement* *Review and revise plan as needed*

Adapted from: Walker, Colvin, & Ramsey, 1995.

Appendices

Appendix	Form	Page	
A	2.1	150	Summary and Checklist for Acting-Out Behavior Cycle
B	2.2	152	Behavior Support Plan
C	3.1	153	Checklist for Evaluating Classroom Space
D	3.2	154	Checklist for Developing a Functional Schedule
E	3.3	155	An Instruction Plan for Teaching Classroom Expectations
F	3.4	156	List of Common Classroom Routines
G	3.5	157	Checklist for Examining Instructional Practices
H	3.6	157	Checklist for Examining Strategies for Intervening During Instruction
I	4.1	158	Precorrection Checklist and Plan
J	8.1	159	Sample Checklist for School Emergency Action Response Plan
K	8.2	160	School Crisis/Emergency Response Checklist
L	8.3	161	School Crisis/Emergency Response Action Plan
M	9.1	162	Behavior Form for Debriefing Process
N	9.2	163	Incident Debriefing Behavior Form
O	10.1	164	Debriefing Form

Appendix A

Form 2.1: Summary and Checklist for Acting-Out Behavior Cycle

Student Name: _____   Date: _____

Home Room Teacher: _____   Grade: _____

Phase One: CALM
Overall behavior is cooperative and acceptable

___ Maintains on-task behavior

___ Follows rules and expectations

___ Responsive to praise

___ Initiates appropriate behavior

___ Goal-oriented

___ Other

Phase Two: TRIGGERS
Overall behavior involves a series of unresolved problems

School-Based

___ Conflicts

   a. Denial of something needed
   b. Something negative is inflicted

___ Changes in routine

___ Peer provocations

___ Pressure

___ Ineffective problem solving

___ Facing errors in instruction

___ Facing correction procedures

___ Other

Nonschool-Based

___ High needs homes

___ Health problems

___ Nutrition needs

___ Inadequate sleep

___ Dual diagnoses

___ Substance abuse

___ Gangs and deviant peer groups

___ Compound triggers

___ Other

Phase Three: AGITATION
Overall behavior is unfocused and distracted

Increases in Behavior

___ Darting eyes

___ Busy hands

___ Moving in and out of groups

___ Off-task and on-task cycle

___ Other

Decreases in Behavior

___ Staring into space

___ Veiled eyes

___ Nonconversational language

___ Contained hands

___ Withdrawal from groups

___ Other

Continued next page.

Geoff Colvin

Phase Four: ACCELERATION

Overall behavior is staff-engaging leading to further negative interactions

____ Questioning and arguing

____ Noncompliance and defiance

____ Off-task behavior

____ Provocation of others

____ Compliance with accompanying
inappropriate behavior

____ Criterion problems

____ Rule violation

____ Whining and crying

____ Avoidance and escape

____ Threats and intimidation

____ Verbal abuse

____ Destruction of property

____ Other

Phase Five: PEAK

Overall behavior is out of control

____ Serious destruction of property

____ Physical attacks

____ Self-abuse

____ Severe tantrums

____ Running away

____ Other

Phase Six: DE-ESCALATION

Overall behavior shows confusion and lack of focus

____ Confusion

____ Reconciliation

____ Withdrawal

____ Denial

____ Blaming others

____ Responsiveness to directions

____ Responsiveness to manipulative or
mechanical tasks

____ Avoidance of discussion

____ Avoidance of debriefing

____ Other

Phase Seven: RECOVERY

Overall behavior shows an eagerness for busy work and a reluctance to interact

____ Eagerness for independent work
or activity

____ Subdued behavior in group work

____ Subdued behavior in class
discussions

____ Defensive behavior

____ Other

© Behavior Associates. Permission to reproduce for personal use.   *Adapted from:* Walker, Colvin, & Ramsey, *1995.*

Form 2.2: Behavior Support Plan

Student Name:	Date:
Home Room Teacher:	Grade:
Staff Present:	

ASSESSMENT	STRATEGIES
Calm	Calm
Triggers	Triggers
Agitation	Agitation
Acceleration	Acceleration
Peak	Peak
De-escalation	De-escalation
Recovery	Recovery

Appendix C

Form 3.1: Checklist for Evaluating Classroom Space

Activity	Completion Date	Notes
1. Locate specific classroom areas for:		_____
a. Independent work	___/___/___	_____
b. Group work	___/___/___	_____
c. Free activity	___/___/___	_____
d. Time out	___/___/___	_____
e. Materials storage	___/___/___	_____
f. Notice board	___/___/___	_____
g. Quiet area	___/___/___	_____
h. Other	___/___/___	_____
2. Draw up seating plans:		_____
a. Rows	___/___/___	_____
b. Clusters	___/___/___	_____
c. Semicircular	___/___/___	_____
d. Other	___/___/___	_____
3. Identify other classroom design tasks	___/___/___	_____
_____		_____
_____		_____
_____		_____
_____		_____

Source: Colvin & Lazar (1997), 108.

Appendix D

Form 3.2: Checklist for Developing a Functional Schedule

Activity	Completion Date	Notes
1. Identify school-wide fixed schedules for:		_____
a. Start of school day	__/__/__	_____
b. Morning recess	__/__/__	_____
c. Lunch	__/__/__	_____
d. Afternoon recess	__/__/__	_____
e. End of school day	__/__/__	_____
f. Other	__/__/__	_____
2. Identify specialist schedule:		
a. Music	__/__/__	_____
b. Art	__/__/__	_____
c. Library	__/__/__	_____
d. Physical education	__/__/__	_____
e. Labs	__/__/__	_____
f. Other	__/__/__	_____
3. Identify team teaching periods	__/__/__	_____
4. Develop classroom schedule for:		_____
a. Master schedule	__/__/__	_____
b. First day	__/__/__	_____
c. First week	__/__/__	_____
d. First month	__/__/__	

Source: Colvin & Lazar (1997), 110.

Geoff Colvin

Form 3.3: An Instruction Plan for Teaching Classroom Expectations

Expected Behavior:
Step One: **Explain**
Step Two: **Specify Student Behaviors**
Step Three: **Practice**
Step Four: **Monitor**
Step Five: **Review**

Adapted from: Colvin & Lazar (1997), 17–18.

Appendix F

Form 3.4: List of Common Classroom Routines

___ Starting the day or the period
___ Entering the classroom
___ Working independently
___ Securing assistance
___ Organizing and managing assignments
___ Conducting tests and quizzes
___ Speaking in class
___ Sending work home
___ Moving around the classroom
___ Establishing class helpers
___ Obtaining supplies
___ Using the restroom
___ Using the water fountain
___ Meeting special needs
___ Using filler activities

Appendix G

Form 3.5: Checklist for Examining Instructional Practices

___ Instructional objectives specified

___ Teaching to mastery practiced

___ Continuous academic measures are employed

___ Instruction is geared to student success (approximately 75-80% success for new learning)

___ Students are successful at the rate of at least 90% for independent work

___ Students are engaged in on-task work quickly

___ Students are given opportunities to respond at a reasonable rate

___ Planned variation of instruction is used

___ Lesson activity flow is maintained

___ Academic learning time is maximized

___ Systematic error correction procedures are used

___ Student feedback on assignments turned in is reasonably quick

Appendix H

Form 3.6: Checklist for Examining Strategies for Intervening During Instruction

___ Establish an entry activity and prompt students to engage quickly

___ Make initial explanations brief

___ Secure all students' attention before giving explanations

___ Plan for difficult transitions

___ Use direct speech

___ Avoid dead time

___ Settle students down at the end of the period

Form 4.1: Precorrection Checklist and Plan

Student Name: Date:

Home Room Teacher: Grade:

_____ 1. Context

_____   Problem Behavior

_____ 2. Expected Behavior

_____ 3. Context Modification

_____ 4. Behavior Rehearsal

_____ 5. Strong Reinforcement

_____ 6. Prompts

_____ 7. Monitoring Plan

© Behavior Associates.   Permission to reproduce for personal use.

Appendix J

Form 8.1: Sample Checklist for School Emergency Action Response Plan

1. Immediate

____ Assess life and safety issues immediately.

____ Provide immediate emergency care as needed.

____ Call 911 and notify police (and rescue people as needed).

____ Secure all areas.

____ Alert school staff of the situation with directions for their roles.

____ Implement protection procedures as necessary such as lock-down or evacuation.

____ Implement dismissal procedures as planned, if needed.

____ Contact school district office, especially the superintendent.

2. Within the First Hour

____ Convene the crisis team to ensure immediate steps have been taken and then identify all the necessary subsequent steps to be followed, designating the person in charge of each step.

____ Identify necessary and available resources that need to be utilized.

____ Implement communication procedures.

____ Alert persons in charge of communications, especially to avoid confusion and misinformation.

____ Notify parents and appropriate community agencies.

____ Contact district public relations office and prepare a measured statement for public dissemination.

Appendix K

Form 8.2: School Crisis/Emergency Response Checklist[1]

Date of Assessment:
Person(s) Completing Assessment:
Check status of each item (in place, partially in place, not in place).

In-Place Status			
Fully	Partially	Not	Item
			1. Crisis response team identified
			2. Home-school-community linkage
			3. Proactive school-wide discipline system
			4. High rates of academic & social success
			5. Clear written policy & procedures
			6. Regular, supervised opportunities to practice (staff and students)
			7. Posted generic response sequence
			8. Designated safe areas
			9. Clear roles & responsibilities of key personnel
			10. Clear fool-proof communication system
			11. Means of securing immediate external support
			12. Procedures for securing or locking down classroom or school
			13. Posted instructions for unique situations
			14. Procedures for accounting for whereabouts of all students & staff
			15. Systematic process for conducting investigations
			16. Clear policy on physical interventions
			17. Procedures for documenting dangerous & potentially dangerous situations

[1]Complete checklist at least quarterly.

Source: Sugai & Colvin, 1999.

Appendix L

Form 8.3: School Crisis/Emergency Response Action Plan

<table>
<tr><td colspan="4">Team Present in Developing Action Plan:</td></tr>
<tr><td>1. Overall status</td><td>High</td><td>Medium</td><td>Low</td></tr>
<tr><td>2. List three major strengths</td><td colspan="3">a.

b.

c.</td></tr>
<tr><td>3. List three major areas in need of improvement

4. Circle the area <u>most</u> in need of improvement</td><td colspan="3">a.

b.

c.</td></tr>
<tr><td>5. Develop an <u>Action Plan</u> for circled area</td><td colspan="3">Step 1:   Who:_____ When:_____

Step 2:   Who:_____ When:_____

Step 3:   Who:_____ When:_____

Step 4:   Who:_____ When:_____

Step 5:   Who:_____ When:_____

Step 6:   Who:_____ When:_____</td></tr>
<tr><td>6. Schedule next self-assessment</td><td colspan="3">Who:_____   When: _____</td></tr>
</table>

Source: Sugai & Colvin, 1999.

Appendix M

Form 9.1: Behavior Form for Debriefing Process

Student Name: _____ Date: _____

1. What was your behavior?

   _____

   _____

   _____

2. What was your concern or need?

   _____

   _____

   _____

3. What could you do next time that would be acceptable?

   _____

   _____

   _____

4. What are you expected to do next?

   _____

   _____

   _____

5. Can you do it appropriately?   ___ Yes ___ No

   Student signature _____

   Teacher signature _____

Source: Walker, Colvin, & Ramsey, 1995.

Geoff Colvin

Appendix N

Form 9.2: Incident Debriefing Behavior Form

Student Name: _____ Date: _____

1. What was your behavior?

   _____

   _____

2. What did you want?
   ___ I wanted attention from others
   ___ I wanted to be in control of the situation
   ___ I wanted to challenge the teacher
   ___ I wanted to avoid doing my work
   ___ I wanted to be sent home
   ___ I wanted to cause problems because I am having a bad day
   ___ I wanted to get back at others because they don't like me
   ___ I wanted revenge
   ___ I wanted_____

3. Did you get what you wanted?   ___ Yes ___ No

   Explain _____

   _____

   _____

4. What are you required to do next?_____

   _____

   _____

5. Will you be able to do it appropriately?   ___ Yes ___ No

   Why? _____

   _____

   Signature: _____

Time started:	Time ended:
Given by:	Number of minutes:
Reviewed by:	Time added:
Class:	**Total time owed:**

Appendix O

Form 10.1: Debriefing Form

Student Name: Grade: Room:

Classroom Teacher: Date:

Staff Member conducting debriefing session
(if different from Classroom Teacher):

1. What did **you** do? _____

_____

_____

_____

2. What, when, and why did the problem occur? _____

_____

_____

_____

3. What will <u>you </u>do next time instead of the problem behavior? _____

_____

_____

_____

4. What do you need to do next after we complete this form? _____

_____

_____

_____

5. Do you need help to take the next step? _____

_____

_____

_____

Student Signature_____   Staff Signature_____

© Behavior Associates. Permission to reproduce for personal use.

References

Achenbach, T. M. (1991). *The child behavior checklist: Manual for the teacher's report form.* Burlington: University of Vermont, Department of Psychiatry.

Bower, G. H. (1992). How might emotions affect learning? In S. Christianson (Ed.), *The handbook of emotion and memory: Research and theory* (pp. 3–32). Hillsdale, NJ: Erlbaum.

Burns, B. J., Schoenwald, S. K., Burchard, J. D., Faw, L., & Santos, A. B. (2000). Comprehensive community-based interventions for youth with severe emotional disorders: Multisystemic therapy and the wraparound process. *Journal of Child and Family Studies, 9,* 283–314.

Canady, R. L., & Rettig, M. D. (Eds.). (1996). *Teaching in the block: Strategies for engaging active learners.* Larchmont, NY: Eye on Education.

Carr, E. G., & Durand, V. M. (1985). Reducing behavior problems through functional communication training. *Journal of Applied Behavior Analysis, 18,* 111–126.

Colvin, G. (1992). *Managing acting-out behavior: A staff development program to prevent and manage acting-out behavior* (Video program). Longmont, CO: Sopris West.

Colvin, G. (1999). *Defusing anger and aggression: Safe strategies for secondary school educators* (Video program). Eugene, OR: Iris Media.

Colvin, G. (2001). *Managing threats: A school-wide action plan* (Video program). Eugene, OR: Iris Media.

Colvin, G., Greenberg, S., & Sherman, R. (1993). Improving academic skills for students with serious emotional disturbances: The forgotten variable. In J. Marr, G. Sugai, & G. Tindal (Eds.), *The Oregon conference monograph 1993* (pp. 9–14). Eugene: University of Oregon, College of Education.

Colvin, G., Kame'enui, E., & Sugai, G. (1993). School-wide and classroom management: Reconceptualizing the integration and management of students with behavior problems in general education. *Education and Treatment of Children, 16,* 361–381.

Colvin, G., & Lazar, M. (1997). *The effective elementary classroom: Managing for success.* Longmont, CO: Sopris West.

Colvin, G., & Sugai, G. (1988). Proactive strategies for managing social behavior problems: An instructional approach. *Education and Treatment of Children, 11*(4), 341–348.

Colvin, G., Sugai, G., & Patching, W. (1993). Pre-correction: An instructional approach for managing predictable problem behaviors. *Intervention in School and Clinic, 28,* 143–150.

Cotton, K. (1990). Schoolwide and classroom discipline. *School improvement research series: Close-up #9.* Portland, OR: Northwest Regional Educational Laboratory.

Crowe, T. D. (1990, Fall). Designing safe schools. *School Safety,* 9–13.

Darch, C. B., & Kame'enui, E. (2004). *Instructional classroom management: A proactive approach to behavior management* (2nd ed.). Upper Saddle River, NJ: Prentice Hall.

Dwyer, K., Osher, D., & Warger, C. (1998). *Early warning, timely response: A guide to safe schools.* Washington, DC: U.S. Department of Education.

Eber, L. (1997). Improving school-based behavioral interventions through use of the wraparound process. *Journal of Reaching Today's Youth, 1*(2), 32–36.

Eber, L. (1999). Family voice, teacher voice: Finding common ground through the wraparound process. *Claiming Children.* Alexandria, VA: The Federation of Families for Children's Mental Health.

Eber, L., Sugai, G., Smith, C., & Scott, T. (2002). Wraparound and positive behavioral interventions and supports in the schools. *Journal of Emotional and Behavior Disorders, 10*(3), 171–180.

Eggert, L. (2001). *Managing anger skills training (MAST).* Bloomington, IN: National Educational Service.

Embry, D. D., & Flannery, D. J. (1994). *Peacebuilders—Reducing youth violence: A working application of cognitive-social-imitative competence research.* Tucson, AZ: Heartsprings, Inc.

Emmer, E. T., Evertson, C. M., Clements, B. S., & Worsham, M. E. (1994). *Classroom management for secondary teachers.* Boston: Allyn and Bacon.

Engelmann, S., & Carnine, D. (1982). *Theory of instruction: Principles and applications.* New York: Irvington.

Engelmann, S., & Colvin, G. (1983). *Generalized compliance training: A direct-instruction program for managing severe behavior problems.* Austin, TX: PRO-ED.

Engelmann, S., & Steely, D. (2004). *Inferred functions of performance and learning.* Mahwah, NJ: Lawrence Erlbaum Associates.

Evans, I. M., & Meyer, L. H. (1985). *An educative approach to behavior problems: A practical design model for interventions with severely handicapped learners.* Baltimore: Paul H. Brookes.

Goldstein, A., Glick, B., & Gibbs, J. (1998). *Aggression replacement training: A comprehensive intervention for aggressive youth.* Champaign, IL: Research Press.

Gresham, F. (2002). Social skills assessment and instruction. In K. L. Lane, F. Gresham, & T. O'Shaughnessy (Eds.), *Interventions for children with or at risk for emotional and behavioral disorders.* Boston: Allyn and Bacon.

Gresham, F., & Elliott, S. N. (1990). *Social Skills Rating System (SSRS).* Circle Pines, MN: American Guidance.

Gresham, F., Sugai, G., & Horner, R. H. (2001). Social competence of students with high-incidence disabilities: Conceptual and methodological issues in interpreting outcomes of social skills training. *Exceptional Children, 67,* 331–344.

Hawkins, D., & Catalano, R. (1992). *Communities that care.* San Francisco: Jossey-Bass.

Hofmeister, A., & Lubke, M. (1990). *Research into practice.* Boston: Allyn and Bacon.

Holm, O. (1997). Ratings of empathic communication: Does experience make a difference? *The Journal of Psychology, 3,* 680–689.

Horner, R. H., & Billingsley, F. F. (1988). The effect of competing behavior on the generalization and maintenance of adaptive behavior in applied settings. In R. H. Horner, G. Dunlap, & R. L. Koegel (Eds.), *Generalization and maintenance: Lifestyle changes in applied settings* (pp. 197–220). Baltimore: Paul H. Brookes.

Horner, R. H., Sugai, G., & Horner, H. F. (2000). A schoolwide approach to student discipline. *The School Administrator, 57*(2), 20–23.

Huggins, P. (1998). *Helping kids handle anger: Teaching self-control.* Longmont, CO: Sopris West.

Isen, A. M. (1984). Toward understanding the role of affect in cognition. In R. S. Wyer Jr. & T. K. Srull (Eds.), *Handbook of motivation and cognition* (Vol. 3, pp. 179–236). Hillsdale, NJ: Lawrence Erlbaum.

Kame'enui, E., & Simmons, D. (1990). *Designing instructional strategies: The prevention of academic and learning difficulties.* Columbus, OH: Charles E. Merrill.

Kauffman, J. M. (2001). *Characteristics of emotional and behavior disorders of children and youth* (7th ed.). Columbus, OH: Merrill.

Kauffman, J. M., Mostert, M. P., Trent, S. C., & Hallahan, D. P. (1998). *Managing classroom behavior: A reflective case-based approach.* Boston: Allyn and Bacon.

Kupersmidt, J., Coie, J., & Dodge, K. (1990). The role of peer relationships in the development of disorder. In S. Asher & J. Coie (Eds.), *Peer rejection in childhood* (pp. 274–308). New York: Cambridge University Press.

Mace, F. C. (1996). In pursuit of general behavioral relations. *Journal of Applied Behavior Analysis, 29*, 557–563.

Mace, F. C., Hock, M. L., Lalli, J. S., West, B. J., Belfiore, P., Pinter, E., & Brown, D. K. (1988). Behavioral momentum in the treatment of noncompliance. *Journal of Applied Behavior Analysis, 21*(2), 123–141.

Malloy, J., Cheney, D., & Cormier, G. (1998). Interagency collaboration and the transition to adulthood for students with emotional or behavioral disabilities. *Education and Treatment of Children, 1*(3), 303–320.

Nelson, J. R., Roberts, M. L., & Smith, D. (1998). *Conducting functional behavioral assessment: A practical guide.* Longmont, CO: Sopris West.

O'Neill, R., Horner, R., Albin, R., Storey, K., Sprague, J., & Newton, J. S. (1997). *Functional assessment and program development for problem behavior: A practical handbook* (2nd ed.). Pacific Grove, CA: Brooks/Cole.

Paine, C., & Sprague, J. (2000). Crisis prevention and response: Is your school prepared? *Oregon School Study Council, 43*(2). Eugene: Institute on Violence and Destructive Behavior, University of Oregon.

Patterson, G. (1988). Family process: Loops, levels, and linkages. In N. Bolger, A. Caspi, G. Downey, & M. Moorehouse (Eds.), *Persons in context: Developmental processes* (pp. 114–151). New York: Cambridge University Press.

Patterson, G. R., Reid, J. B., & Dishion, T. J. (1992). *Antisocial boys: Vol. 4. A social interactional approach.* Eugene, OR: Castalia.

Plake, B. S., Impara, J. C., & Spies, R. A. (Eds.). (2003). *The fifteenth mental measurements yearbook.* Lincoln: Buros Institute of Mental Measurement, University of Nebraska.

Rhode, G., Jenson, W., & Reavis, H. K. (1992). *The tough kid book: Practical classroom management strategies.* Longmont, CO: Sopris West.

Sanchez-Fort, M., Brady, M., & Davis, C. (1995). Analysis of a high-probability instructional sequence and time-out in the treatment of noncompliance. *Journal of Applied Behavior Analysis, 27*, 327–330.

Schrumpf, F., Crawford, D., & Usadel, H. (1991). *Peer mediation: Conflict resolution in schools.* Champaign, IL: Research Press.

Singer, G., Singer, J., & Horner, R. (1987). Using pretask requests to increase the probability of compliance for students with severe disabilities. *The Journal of the Association for Persons with Severe Handicaps, 12*(4), 287–291.

Sprague, J., Colvin, G., Irvin, L., & Stieber, S. (1997). *The Oregon school safety survey.* Eugene: Institute on Violence and Destructive Behavior, University of Oregon.

Sprague, J., & Golly, A. (2004). *Best behavior: Building positive behavior supports in schools.* Longmont, CO: Sopris West.

Sprague, J., Sugai, G., & Walker, H. (1998). Antisocial Behavior in Schools. In S. Watson & F. M. Gresham (Eds.), *Handbook of Child Behavior Therapy* (pp. 451–474). New York: Plenum Press.

Sprick, R., Garrison, M., & Howard, L. (1998). *CHAMPs: A proactive and positive approach to classroom management.* Longmont, CO: Sopris West.

Sprick, R., Howard, L., Wise, B. J., Marcum, K., & Haykin, M. (1998). *The library: Management, motivation, and discipline.* Longmont, CO: Sopris West.

Stephens, R. D. (1995). *Safe Schools: A handbook for violence prevention.* Bloomington, IN: National Education Service.

Stetter, G. M. T. (1995). *The effects of precorrection on cafeteria behavior.* Unpublished manuscript, University of Virginia, Charlottesville.

Stroul, B. A. (1993). *Systems of care for children and adolescents with severe emotional disturbances: What are the results?* Washington, DC: CASSP Technical Assistance Center, Center for Child Health and Mental Health Policy, and Georgetown University Child Development Center.

Sugai, G., & Colvin, G. (1997). Debriefing: A transition step for promoting acceptable behavior. *Education and Treatment of Children, 20,* 209–221.

Sugai, G., & Colvin, G. (1999). *Primer on crises and emergency responses.* Eugene: PBIS, College of Education, University of Oregon.

Sugai, G., Horner, R. H., & Gresham, F. M. (2002). Behaviorally effective school environments. In M. Shinn, H. M. Walker, & M. Stoner (Eds.), *Interventions for academic and behavior problems II: Preventive and remedial approaches* (pp. 315–350). Bethesda, MD: NASP Publications.

Sugai, G., Kame'enui, E., & Colvin, G. (1993). *Project PREPARE: Promoting responsible, empirical, and proactive alternatives in regular education for students with behavior disorders.* Eugene: Technical Report, University of Oregon.

Sugai, G., & Lewis, T. (1996). Preferred and promising practices for social skills instruction. *Focus on Exceptional Children, 29,* 1–16.

Walker, H. M., Colvin, G., & Ramsey, E. (1995). *Antisocial behavior in schools: Strategies and best practices.* Pacific Grove, CA: Brooks/Cole.

Walker, H. M., Kavanagh, K., Stiller, B., Golly, A., Severson, H., & Feil, E. (1995). *The first step to success.* Longmont, CO: Sopris West.

Walker, H. M., & McConnell, S. R. (1993). *The Walker-McConnell scale of social competence and school adjustment* (rev. ed.). Eugene: Center on Human Development, University of Oregon.

Walker, H. M., Stieber, S., Ramsey, E., O'Neill, R. E., & Eisert, D. (1994). Psychological correlates of at-risk status among adolescent boys: Static and dynamic relationships. *Remedial and Special Education.*

Watson, R., Poda, J., Miller, C., Rice, E., & West, G. (1990). *Containing crises: A guide to managing school emergencies.* Bloomington, IN: National Education Service.

Wong, H. K., & Wong, R. T. (1991). *The first days of school: How to be an effective teacher.* Sunnyvale, CA: Harry K. Wong Publications.

Wood, F. H. (1990). When we talk with children: The life space interview. *Behavioral Disorders, 15,* 110–126.

Yasutake, D. T. (1995). The influence of affect on the achievement and behavior of students with learning disabilities. *Journal of Learning Disabilities, 28,* 329–336.

Author Index

Achenbach, T. M., 75
Albin, R., 83

Belfiore, P., 133
Billingsley, F. F., 64, 66
Bower, G. H., 125
Brady, M., 133
Brown, D. K., 133
Burchard, J. D., 83
Burns, B. J., 83

Canady, R. L., 48
Carnine, D., 56, 65, 80
Carr, E. G., 64
Catalano, R., 117
Cheney, D., 85
Clements, B. S., 49, 52
Coie, J., 72
Colvin, G., 12, 36, 44, 49, 50,
    52, 54, 55, 56, 60, 61, 64,
    65, 69, 72, 73, 75, 76, 77,
    98, 105, 110, 114, 116,
    118, 121, 122, 123, 129,
    136
Cormier, G., 85
Cotton, K., 46
Crawford, D., 81
Crowe, T. D., 117, 123

Darch, C. B., 52
Davis, C., 133
Dishion, T. J., 12
Dodge, K., 72
Durand, V. M., 64
Dwyer, K., 115, 118, 123

Eber, L., 83, 84, 85
Eggert, L., 81
Eisert, D., 12
Elliott, S. N., 75
Embry, D. D., 118, 123
Emmer, E. T., 49, 52
Engelmann, S., 56, 60, 64, 65,
    80
Evans, I. M., 64
Evertson, C. M., 49, 52

Faw, L., 83
Feil, E., 81
Flannery, D. J., 118, 123

Garrison, M., 49
Gibbs, J., 81
Glick, B., 81
Goldstein, A., 81
Golly, A., 12, 44, 56, 81
Greenberg, S., 56
Gresham, F., 72, 73, 74, 75, 77,
    79, 83

Hallahan, D. P., 12, 49, 60, 73
Hawkins, D., 117
Haykin, M., 52
Hock, M. L., 133
Hofmeister, A., 49
Holm, O., 97
Horner, H. F., 118, 123
Horner, R. H., 64, 66, 72, 73,
    79, 83, 118, 123, 133
Howard, L., 49, 52
Huggins, P., 81

Impara, J. C., 81
Irvin, L., 114
Isen, A. M., 125

Jenson, W., 81

Kame'enui, E., 52, 118
Kauffman, J. M., 12, 49, 52,
    60, 61, 69, 73
Kavanagh, K., 81
Kupersmidt, J., 72

Lalli, J. S., 133
Lazar, M., 44, 50, 52, 54, 55,
    60, 105
Lewis, T., 72, 74, 49, 80
Lubke, M., 49

Mace, F. C., 133
Malloy, J., 85
Marcum, K., 52
McConnell, S. R., 75
Meyer, L. H., 64
Miller, C., 115, 123
Mostert, M. P., 12, 49, 60, 73

Nelson, J. R., 83
Newton, J. S., 83

O'Neill, R., 12, 83
Osher, D., 115, 118, 123

Paine, C., 114, 118, 119, 123
Patching, W., 60
Patterson, G., 12
Pinter, E., 133
Plake, B. S., 81
Poda, J., 115, 123

Ramsey, E., 12, 36, 49, 72,
    73, 75, 76, 77, 118, 129
Reavis, H. K., 81
Reid, J. B., 12
Rettig, M. D., 48
Rhode, G., 81
Rice, E., 115, 123
Roberts, M. L., 83

Sanchez-Fort, M., 133
Santos, A. B., 83
Schoenwald, S. K., 83
Schrumpf, F., 81
Scott, T., 83, 84, 85

Severson, H., 81
Sherman, R., 56
Simmons, D. I., 61
Singer, G., 133
Singer, J., 133
Smith, C., 83, 84, 85
Smith, D., 83
Spies, R. A., 81
Sprague, J., 12, 44, 56, 72, 73,
    83, 114, 118, 119, 123
Sprick, R., 49, 52
Steely, D., 56, 60, 65, 80
Stephens, R. D., 115, 118, 123
Stetter, G. M. T., 61
Stieber, S., 12, 44
Stiller, B., 81
Storey, K., 83
Stroul, B. A., 85
Sugai, G., 52, 60, 61, 65, 69,
    72, 73, 74, 79, 80, 83,
    84, 85, 110, 116, 118,
    121, 122, 123, 136

Trent, S. C., 12, 49, 60, 73

Usadel, H., 81

Walker, H., 12, 36, 49, 72,
    73, 75, 76, 77, 81, 83,
    118, 129
Warger, C., 115, 118, 123
Watson, R., 115, 123
West, B. J., 133
West, G., 115, 123
Wise, B. J., 52
Wong, H. K., 49
Wong, R. T., 49
Wood, F. H., 137
Worsham, M. E., 49, 52

Yasutake, D. T., 125, 127

SUBJECT INDEX

Abuse
  high needs homes and, 19
  of self, peak phase and, 29
  of substances, nonschool-
    based triggers and, 20
Academic skills
  as deterrent to violence, 118
  as prerequisite, 7
Acceleration phase
  characteristics of, 25–29,
  defusing strategies for, 98–
    113
Accommodation strategies,
  86–97
  peer perception, fairness
    of, 95–97
  teacher empathy and, 87
Achenbach Child Behavior
  Checklist, 75
Acknowledgment of
  problem-solving
  behaviors, 135
Acting-out behavior cycle
  analysis of, 4–11
  assessment form for, 38–39
  example of, 4–7
  seven-phase model, 12–41,
    144–147
  strategies for
    management, 44–141
Agitation phase
  calming strategies for, 86–
    97
  characteristics of, 7–8, 12,
    22–25
  timing of
    accommodations, 87
Anger, peak phase and, 29–30

Antisocial behavior
  agitation levels and, 12
  cool-down time
    variability, 126
  individual programming
    for, 82–85
  outcomes for displays of,
    73–74
  social skills curricula for, 81
Arguing, acceleration phase
  and, 25
Assault, peak phase and, 29
Assessment
  curriculum planning and,
    56
  functional, 63
  of social skills, 75–78
Assessment form, 37–39
Avoidance,
  of debriefing, 32
  of escalating prompts,
    posture as intervention
    strategy, 98–99
  and escape, 27
  of task, 96

Behavior
  cluster, response class
    and, 77
  direct observations of, 76–
    78
  documentation, 128–133
  management strategies,
    44–141
  ownership, 131
  student self-management
    of, 93

Behavior chain. *See*
  Escalating behavior
  chain
Behavior disorders, emotional
  and, (EBD), 83
Behavior expectations
  behavior support plan 37–
    40,
  communicating to
    students, 50–52, 135–
    136
  prompting of, 67
  specifying, 63–64
  strong reinforcement of, 66
  student decision and, 105
Behavior rehearsals, 65–66
Behavior form
  sample of, 129, 130
  student completion of,
    128, 131–132
Behavior problems,
  precorrection, 62–69
Behavior rating scales, 75–76
Behavior support plan, 37–
  40, 144–146
Blaming others, de-escalation
  phase and, 31
*Buros Mental Measurement
  Yearbook*, 75
Busy hands, agitation phase
  and, 23

Calming strategies, agitation
  phase and, 86–97
Calmness, posture as
  intervention strategy,
  100–101

Calm phase
    characteristics of, 14–15,
    proactive strategies for,
    44–58
Case study, 39–40, 69–70,
    145–147
Changes, in routine as
    school-based trigger, 18
Checklists, 151, 153, 154, 157–
    160
    precorrection plan and,
    67–70
Child abuse/neglect,
    nonschool-based
    triggers and, 19
Choice activities, classroom
    arrangement and, 45
Classroom environment
    disruption of, 29–30, 114,
    116
    learning environment, 44–
    58
    notice board, 46
    physical design of, calm
    phase and, 44–47
    restoration of, 132–133
Classroom expectations, 49–
    52, 95–96
    establishing, 50–52
    function of, 50–51
    instruction plan for, 51
    secondary students and,
    52
    two sets, fairness and, 95–
    96
Classroom management
    calm phase and, 44–58
    routines, proactive, 53–55
    rules, establishing, 50–52
    schedule, establishing, 48–
    49
Community personnel
    coordination of for school
    safety, 117
    wraparound process and,
    83–85
Compliance
    vs. consequence, 104–112
    delayed, 109–110
    partial and non-, 26–27

Conflicts, as school-based
    trigger, 16–17
Confusion, de-escalation
    phase and, 31, 127
Consequences
    as choice, prompting
    behaviors and, 67
    determination of, 132–133
    establishing, 104–105
    non-negotiability of, 135
Context
    identification, 63
    modification, 64–65
Cool-down time, 126, 128
Cooperation, de-escalation
    phase and, 32, 127–128
Correction procedures
    as consequent
    manipulations, 61
    as school-based trigger,
    18–19
Crisis prevention, staff
    training, 118
Criterion problems,
    acceleration phase and,
    27
Crying, acceleration phase
    and, 27
Curriculum planning, 56

Darting eyes, agitation phase
    and, 23
Debriefing
    form, 128–131, 139, 140
    as intervention strategy,
    110–112, 131, 136–141
    session guidelines, 137–138
    student avoidance of, 32
De-escalation phase
    characteristics of, 31–33
    reintegration strategies
    for, 125–133
Defensiveness, recovery
    phase and, 33
Defiance, acceleration phase
    and, 25–26
Defusing strategies, 98–113
Delayed compliance, 109–110

Denial, de-escalation phase
    and, 31
Destruction of property
    acceleration phase and, 28
    peak phase and, 29, 114
Detachment posture, 100–101
Deviant peer groups as
    nonschool-based
    trigger, 20
Direct observations
    guidelines, 76
    of operationally defined
    behaviors, 76
    recording dimensions, 76–
    77
Documentation of behavior
    problems, 128–133
Drug abuse as nonschool-
    based trigger, 20
Dual diagnoses,
    complications of as
    trigger, 20
Dysfunctional homes as
    nonschool-based
    trigger, 19

Emergency situation
    district policy, 115
    follow up, 117, 119–120, 123
    identification, 115–116
    prerequisites, 117
    preventing, 114–119
    procedures, 116–118
    review, 117
    tracking, 117
Empathy, agitation phase
    and, 87
Encouragement, 135–136
Engaging behaviors
    disengaging, set response,
    99
    student–staff, 25–29, 98–107
Environment. See also
    Classroom
    environment
    restoration of, 132–133
Error correction, as school-
    based trigger, 18–19

Escalating behavior chain
avoiding escalating
prompts in, 98–99
example of, 6, 8
presence of, 8–9
successive interactions
and, 9–11
Escalating prompts, avoidance
strategy, 98–99
Escape behavior, acceleration
phase and, 29–30
Exit interview, 137
Exit paperwork, 128–131
Expectations, classroom. *See*
Cassroom expectations
Eyes in agitation phase
darting, 23
staring into space, 23
veiled, 23

Fairness
accommodation strategy
and, 94–95
student privileges and,
95–96
Families
high needs, as nonschool-
based trigger, 19
wraparound process and,
83–85
Feedback
with praise, 67, 135–136
session, 137
Focus
as agitation strategy, 87
on cooperation, 127–133
as de-escalation strategy,
127–128
on normal routines, 134–
135
Follow through,
consequences, 108–109
Forms, 150–164
Free-time activities,
classroom arrangement
and, 45

Functional assessment
behavior and context
identification, 63
individual programming
and, 82–83
Functional replacement
behavior, 64

Gang affiliation as trigger, 20
Gestures, use in prompting
behavior, 67
Goal orientation, calm phase
and, 14–15
Group involvement
isolation from, 126
joining, 23
withdrawal, 24
Group work
classroom arrangement
and, 45
subdued, recovery phase
and, 33

Hands in agitation phase
busy, 23
containment of, 24
Harrassment of others, 26
Health factors as nonschool-
based trigger, 19
Home, high needs as trigger,
19
Hyperventilation, peak
phase and, 29

Independent activities
agitation phase and, 91–92
busy work, 33
classroom arrangement
and, 45
as de-escalation strategy,
127–128
mastery of task, 128
standard for completion,
128
task selection, 128

Individual programming
functional assessments,
82–83
wraparound process, 83–85
Information delivery, 56–57
Instruction
effective delivery of, 56–57
intervening during, 57
management of as
proactive strategy, 44,
55–58
student assessment and, 56
Instructional objectives, 56–57
Interactions, escalating, 9–11
Intervention strategies. *See
specific strategy:*
Acceleration phase;
Agitation phase; Calm
phase; De-escalation
phase; Peak phase;
Recovery phase;
Triggers phase
Intimidation, acceleration
phase and, 28
Isolation as intervention
strategy, 126

Language,
nonconversational,
agitation phase and, 23
Likert rating scales, 75
Limit setting, procedures,
nonconfrontational,
103–110
Limit testing, acceleration
phase and, 26–27
Long-term interventions,
peak-phase behavior
and, 123

Medication, side effects as
triggers, 20
Model, conceptual, 12–41
Monitoring
emergency situations, 117,
123
precorrection plan and,
67–70

Movement activities, agitation strategies and, 92

Negative consequences
establishing, 104–108
follow through, 108–109
and problem behavior cycle, 136
Neighborhood factors and school safety, 117
Noncompliance. *See also* Compliance
acceleration phase and, 25–26, 110–112
Nonconfrontational limit-setting procedures, 103–110
Nonconversational language, agitation phase and, 23
Nonschool-based triggers, 19–22
Nonthreatening approach, 101–102
Notice board, classroom arrangement and, 46
Nutrition needs, nonschool-based trigger, 19

Observations, direct, social skills assessment and, 75–78
Off-task behavior
acceleration phase and, 26
cycle, agitation phase and, 23
On-task behavior
calm phase and, 14–15
cycle, agitation phase and, 23
recovery phase and, 33
Ownership of behavior, 131, 137

Paperwork, documentation, 128–133

Parents
nonschool-based triggers and, 19
wraparound process and, 83–85, 144
Passive strategies, agitation phase and, 92
Peak phase
characteristics of, 29–30
safe management strategies for, 114–124
Peers
deviant groups of, as nonschool-based triggers, 20
provocation by, as school-based trigger, 18
provocation of, acceleration phase and, 26
Phases. *See specific phases:*
Acceleration phase;
Agitation phase; Calm phase; De-escalation phase; Peak phase;
Recovery phase;
Triggers phase
Physical arrangement, classroom, 44–46
Policy
consistency, 115
educational vision, 115
school/district safety, 115
Practice
emergency procedures, 118, 120
limit-setting procedures, 103–104
Praise, feedback and, 67, 135–136
Precorrection
as antecedent manipulation, 61
vs. correction distinction, 60–61
as instructional tool, 60–61
steps and predictable behavior problems, 62–69
triggers phase and, 59–71

Preferred activities, 90
Prerequisite academic skills, 7
Pressure, as school-based trigger, 18
Privileges, perceived, and fairness, 95–96
Proactive strategies
calm phase and, 44–58
debriefing session as, 137
schoolwide discipline plans, 118
Problem behavior
and negative consequences cycle, 62–69
precorrection and, 62–69
Problem solving
acknowledgment of, 135
difficulties as trigger, 18
meeting, 137
Prompting
expected behaviors, 67
gestures and, 67
Provocation
by peers, triggers phase and, 18
of peers, acceleration phase and, 26

Questioning, acceleration phase and, 25
Quiet area
abuse of, 96
agitation phase and, 89
de-escalation phase and, 126
establishing, 46

Reactive teacher behavior, 100
Reconciliation, de-escalation phase and, 31
Recovery phase
characteristics of, 33–34
resumption strategies for, 134–141
Rehearsal
behavior rehearsals, 65–66
emergency response plan, 118, 120

Rehersal *(continued)*
  limit-setting procedures, 103–104
Reinforcement
  history, 67
  strong reinforcers, 66
Reintegration, de-escalation phase
  process, 18
  strategies, 125–133
Relaxation activities, agitation phase and, 89
Respectful posture intervention strategy, 100–101
Response plan, crisis action, 118–119
Response shaping, 131–132
Responsibility, student ownership, 105–113, 131
Responsiveness de-escalation phase and, 32
Resumption strategies, recovery phase and, 134–141
Review
  emergency situation, 117
  problem incident, 137
Routines
  changes in as triggers, 18
  establishing in classroom, 53–55
  focus on in recovery phase, 134–135
  instructional efficiency, 53
Rule
  compliance, calm phase, 14–15
  violation, acceleration phase, 27

Safe management strategies, guiding principles, 116–117
  peak phase and, 114–124
  safe physical school property, 117
  school/district safety policy, 115

Schedule
  establishing, 46–49
  resumption after incident, 133, 134
School-based triggers, 16–19
Schoolwide safety policy, 115
Seating arrangements, flexibility and, 46
Secondary students, teaching behavior to, 52
Self-abuse, peak phase and, 29
Self-management, as intervention strategy, 93–95, 144
Serious behavior, consequence nonnegotiability, 135
Setting change, recovery phase and, 134
Seven-phase model, description of, 12–41
Sleep problems, nonschool-based trigger, 20
Social competence, defined, 74
Social skills
  assessment procedures, 75–78
  importance of, 72
  rating systems, 75
  terms defined, 74–75
Social skills instruction, 59–60, 72–81
  assumptions underlying, 78–79
  delivering, 80–81
  as precorrective strategy, 72–85
  selecting curricula, 80–81
Space
  organization of, calm phase, 46
  provision of, agitation phase, 88
Staff meeting plan, 144–147
Staring into space, agitation phase and, 23
Stimulus control
  behavior rehearsals and, 65
  context modification and, 64

Storage materials, classroom arrangement and, 45
Strategies. *See specific strategies*
Student isolation as intervention, 126
Student self-management, 93–95, 144
Student success, encouragement of, 135–136
Subdued behavior
  agitation phase and, 23–24
  recovery phase and, 33–34
Substance abuse as nonschool-based trigger, 20
Successive interactions, recognition, 9–11
Supervision, classroom during de-escalation phase, 126
  obstructions and, 46
Suspension after incident, 126–127

Tantrums, peak phase and, 29
Task suitability, 32, 33
Teacher expectations. *See* Classroom expectations
Teacher proximity, agitation phase and, 90–91
Teacher's desk, classroom arrangement and, 45
Teaching social skills
  as intervention strategy, 59–60, 72–81
  triggers phase and, 72–85
Teasing
  acceleration phase and, 26
  as school-based trigger, 18
Threats, acceleration phase and, 28
Time out, classroom arrangement and, 45
Tracking emergency incidents, 117

Transition steps, recovery
    phase, 134–136, 137
Triggers
    compound, 20–22
    defined, 16
    predictable context, 63
    nonschool-based, 19–20
    school-based, 16–19
    student identification of,
        136
Triggers phase
    characteristics of, 16–20
    precorrection strategies
        for, 59–71
    teaching social skills for,
        72–85

Verbal abuse, acceleration
    phase and, 28
Violation of rules, acceleration
    phase and, 27
Violence
    academic achievement as
        deterrent, 118
    peak behavior and, 29, 114

Walker-McConnell Scale of
    Social Competence and
    School Adjustment
    (SSCSA), 75
Whining, acceleration phase
    and, 27

Withdrawal
    from groups, agitation
        phase, 24
    after incident, de-
        escalation phase, 31
    of teacher, posture as
        intervention strategy,
        105–107
Wraparound process
    defined, 84
    environments, 84
    individual programming
        and, 83–85

CREDITS

This page constitutes an extension of the copyright page. Every effort has been made to trace the ownership of copyrighted material and to secure permission from copyright holders. In the event of any issue regarding the use of material in this book, we will be pleased to make any corrections for future printings.

Thanks are due to the following authors, publishers, and agents for permission to use the material indicated.

Chapter 3: Appendix C, Form 3.1; Appendix D, Form 3.2; Appendix E, Form 3.3; Figure 3.2; Box 3.1 and Box 3.3 from *The Effective Elementary Classroom: Managing for Success,* by G. Colvin and M. Lazar. Copyright © 1997 by Sopris West, Longmont, CO. Reprinted and adapted with permission.

Chapter 8: Appendix J, Form 8.1 from *Crisis Prevention and Response: Is your School Prepared?* by C. Paine and J. Sprague. Copyright © 2000 by Institute on Violence and Destructive Behavior, University of Oregon, Eugene. Adapted with permission.

Chapter 8: Appendix K, Form 8.2 from *Primer on Crisis and Emergency Responses,* by G. Sugai and G. Colvin. Copyright © 1999, PBIS, College of Education, University of Oregon, Eugene. Reprinted with permission.

Photos: Credits are due to IRIS Media, Inc., 258 East 10th Ave, Suite B, Eugene, OR, 97401 or www.lookiris.com, for permission to use their numerous copyrighted photos identified throughout the text.

Video Programs

Check Dr. Colvin's Professional Development Video Programs

√ *Managing Non-Compliance: Effective Strategies for K-12 Teachers*

√ *Defusing Anger and Aggression: Safe Strategies for Secondary School Educators*

√ *Managing Threats: A School-Wide Action Plan*

For further information contact:

Behavior Associates
P.O. Box 5633
Eugene OR 97405

Tel: (541) 485-6450
Fax: (541) 344-9680